SINGER AND ACCOMPANIST
The Performance of Fifty Songs

SINGER AND ACCOMPANIST

The Performance of Fifty Songs

by

GERALD MOORE

GREENWOOD PRESS, PUBLISHERS
WESTPORT, CONNECTICUT

Library of Congress Cataloging in Publication Data

Moore, Gerald.
    Singer and accompanist; the performance of fifty
songs.

    Reprint of the 1953 ed. published by Methuen,
London.
    Includes discography for each song.
    1. Singing--Interpretation (Phrasing, dynamics,
etc.) I. Title.
[MT892.M7 1973]   784.9'34   73-11859
ISBN 0-8371-7090-7

Originally published in 1953 by Methuen & Co., Ltd., London

Reprinted with the permission of Methuen & Co., Ltd.

Reprinted in 1973 by Greenwood Press
A division of Congressional Information Service
88 Post Road West, Westport, Connecticut 06881

Library of Congress Catalog Card Number 73-11859

ISBN 0-8371-7090-7

Printed in the United States of America

10 9 8 7

To
ENID

Corrections to Reprint Edition

Page 5, line 7:	*G*eliebte	capital G
Page 11, bar 4:	ho*h*en	insert h
Page 11, bar 5:	se*n*de	insert n
Page 18, line 15:	Brahams'*s*	add s
Page 18, line 17:	Brahams'*s*	add s
Page 23, line 8:	Brahms'*s*	add s
Page 25, line 9:	Brahms'*s*	add s
Page 25, line 30:	Brahms'*s*	add s
Page 31, line 1:	Brahms'*s*	add s
Page 27, bar 46:	S*ch*mach	insert ch
Page 27, bar 48:	*D*ich	capital D
Page 30, line 10:	should read "The *accompaniment* leaps" . . .	
Page 31, line 14:	*L*ebensraum	capital L
Page 66, line 1:	*L*ust	capital L
Page 93, bar 13:	flu*t*tered	insert t
Page 103, line 3:	pré*sent	accent ´
Page 103, line 16:	trè*s	accent `
Page 114, line 5:	"or Ivan the Terrible" to be deleted and "*in his great opera*" inserted instead.	
Page 174, bar 24:	reden trau*n*	separate words, n
Page 217, line 9:	'Benedeit die sel'ge Mutter' to be deleted and '*Schlafendes Jesuskind*' inserted instead.	
Page 219, bar 19:	de*i*ne	ei
Page 220, bar 27:	W*ä*r	add ¨

PREFACE

IT has not been my intention in the following pages to attempt critical analyses of the fifty songs under review (although an analytical note may occasionally have crept in) but rather to explain how the executants might sing and play them; above all to suggest lines they could think along when practising, rehearsing, and performing them. I hope the word 'suggest' will be noted. I have used it advisedly: for there are many roads to heaven and while I am confident that my road will not lead to destruction, I do not claim that it is the *only* way. Let him who disagrees with my ideas make his own investigation and find out what suits him best. I shall be happy if this book has this stimulating effect.

I believe that equal consideration has been given to the two partners, but if more attention than is usual in a book on song interpretation has been bestowed on the accompaniment I make no apology; it has been done for the good of the song and should prove of ultimate benefit to the singer. 'There is no law, human or divine,' said Ernest Newman (in 1907), 'to compel the composer to limit his expressiveness to the voice alone.'

The Schubert, Wolf, Fauré songs (to mention three composers at random) included here can be called great songs. To the question 'What are Beethoven's "Mailied", Rachmaninoff's "Spring Waters", Hahn's "Offrande" doing in such distinguished company?' I would answer that the first song presents difficulties to the singer, the second teases the pianist, while the Hahn song is intriguing if only for its wide dissimilarity to the undeniably finer settings of the same poem by Debussy and Fauré. The only rule I observed when selecting my fifty songs was that they should be interesting; interesting either for their intrinsic worth or for the problems they pose for the singer or the accompanist or both partners.

The reader who is indulgent enough to imagine there is any benefit to be reaped by a study of this book, should dip into it rather than attempt to read it steadily from cover to cover. Let him see which of these songs he possesses and then—after numbering the bars on his score to help him follow me on my wanderings through the song—have his music beside him as he reads. He will thus be in a much better position to laugh with me or at me; to see how unerringly I hit the nail on the head or how lamentable is my aim.

To two great friends I would like to express my deep gratitude: to Mr. L. A. G. Strong for his encouragement and patience ever since he approached me with the idea of this book, and to Mr. Alec Robertson for his invaluable and constructive criticism on its completion.

ACKNOWLEDGEMENTS

I WISH to express my thanks to Miss Astra Desmond and to Messrs. Richard Capell, Martin Cooper, and Ernest Newman for permission to quote from their writings; to Mr. G. Bernard Brophy for his trouble and kindness in the selection of gramophone records; to Noel Douglas Ltd., publishers, for allowing me to reprint the excerpt from 'Monsieur Croche'; and finally to all the publishers—enumerated at the end of each song—for their generous co-operation in allowing me to reprint so many musical illustrations.

London 1953   G.M.

CONTENTS

RECORD MAKES

In the lists at the end of each song the names of the makes of gramophone records are abbreviated as follows:

G	H.M.V.
C	Columbia
D	Decca
P	Parlophone
PD	Polydor
V	Victor
O	Odeon
Pat	Pathé
T	Telefunken
Sco	Scolaphon
ALLO	Allegro
Voc	Vocalion
West	Westminster
IRCC	International Record Collectors' Club
U	Ultraphon
L	Lumen
Sel	Selmer
Van	Vanguard
BaM	Boite à Musique
GSC	Gramophone Shop of N.Y.
Cla	Clangor
OL	Oiseau Lyre
Sch	Schirmer

THE WHITE PEACE

Words by FIONA MACLEOD   *Music by* ARNOLD BAX

ASKED by the characteristically modest Arnold Bax which song he
would choose as a model of perfect song writing, John Coates replied
that anyone taking 'The White Peace' as a paragon would not go far
wrong. This song was a favourite with John McCormack as well as
Coates, and each of these great singers—divergent in style and temperament though they were—brought the same gifts to bear on it: a
perfect *legato* line and perfect enunciation.

This song is all the more difficult to sing because, in fact, it must
sound easy. Each bar is at least of five seconds duration so that great
breath control is needed to last out the phrase and to maintain an
unwavering tone. The listener should be aware of none of these
difficulties, he should be carried away by the music and words. We want
him to be at ease. To suffuse the whole song with 'the moonlight of a
perfect peace' infinite gentleness and calm deliberation are needed to
maintain an unbroken line and a steady stream.

The bountiful range of those opening bars deceives the unwary
singer.

Look at the composer's instructions, '*Piano*. Very quiet.' Obviously
he wants one colour, one quality, one quantity of tone. Do not, then,
allow the low notes in bars 2, 10, and 11 to appear to come from a
different register of the voice than the higher ones. If, for instance, the
first note is taken in the chest, the second in the head voice, this is the
effect you are likely to produce.

I

Yes. It becomes in fact a yodel with a click between the E flat and the C as the voice switches from the chest to the head.

Merely because the first breath is taken after 'hill' (4) and you may be anxious for it, you must not mulct the B flat; it is a full crotchet and wants full value. To ensure this, take time enough for the consonants 'll' to be heard (John McCormack's consonants could almost be seen) and promise yourself a slow, deliberate breath in due course, holding up the time for this breath if need be. On the other hand no one should be aware that a breath is being taken on the quaver rest in 7. With 'main' held for over three beats, 9–10–11 becomes a very long phrase and if it cannot be accomplished in one sweep, a quick imperceptible breath can be taken after 'Nor' in bar 9.

The question posed in the first twelve bars of the song is not answered until the second verse, it is therefore important that the listener should understand every word the singer utters. While it is good in 5 to run the 'r' in 'nor' on to the word 'on' (i.e. 'norron') the same does not apply to 'nor ever', 6–7. 'Ever' is separated from the preceding 'nor'. 'Norrever' is a confusing sound and might be mistaken for 'no never' or 'moreover'. Without altering the value of the notes, get on to the 'nn's' in 'running', bar 8, shortening the vowel. This word is the only one suggestive of motion in the first verse; by stressing the consonants you bring a sense of movement to the word.

It should be noticed that while the vocal line is marked *piano*, the accompaniment is *pianissimo*, and this instruction is very necessary, for the solid-looking chords lie in the most sonorous register of the instrument. They cannot be played too gently. The singer leans on them, feels them like a soft cushion beneath him. Using both the soft and sustaining pedals the pianist floats from one chord to the next with all possible smoothness, being particularly careful not to make the quavers in 5–6 too obtrusive or bumpy.

Ex. 2

If there has been shadow, it is now dissipated in the second verse. Movement is introduced by the syncopation of the left hand ('very quiet') and by the meandering quavers, the shafts of moonlight, in the treble.

Singing from 13 to 18 the same lovely tune he had from 3 to 8 (Ex. 1) the singer still holds the tranquil mood, coloured however by the *crescendo diminuendo*, 14–15, and by the consoling chord on 'pain'. The latter is marked *piano*, and rightly so: for the pain is soothed. Any stabbing accent on this word or a pained expression on the singer's face is entirely out of place (bar 16).

Quaver, semiquaver, triplet decorations in the above example should match the words 'slow moving'. They should be spaced in such a way that while allowing the singer all the time he needs to breathe where a comma is marked, they do not appear to interrupt the even flow of the music.

Only a slight swelling of tone is wanted at 15, for the words here are in parenthesis. It is at 'The moonlight of a perfect peace floods heart and brain' that a new and sudden warmth floods the music.

Of course a breath must be taken before 19 to enable the singer to make that *crescendo* on the long D natural of 20—then a quick breath (which I have marked) to carry over to the word 'peace', (22). Phrase 21 and 22 must be an illuminating and a warming glow, rich with tone. Serenity will be sacrificed, though, unless the singer holds to his *legato* line more securely than ever; especial care is wanted for the quavers in 21. These quavers can be taken *rubato* by staying longer on the G flat and slightly quickening the following three. It is a difficult phrase to sing and by the time he reaches 'peace', 22, the singer will feel relieved, but his relief must not be made evident by the skimping of the word. Indeed 'peace' should be prolonged if possible. The game is up if he can barely reach this point, compelled to shorten his E flat through lack of breath.

There are many wide-stretched chords in the accompaniment which should be spread as little as possible so as not to ruffle the quiet pool of sound. I am in favour of adapting such chords to suit a small hand. Thus, at 17, 18, instead of

Ex. B

we have

Ex. C

which, in my opinion, is preferable to an untidy spreading of the chords. Often the right hand can come to the rescue of the left. Where broken chords are indicated, however, they should be played unhurriedly (the last chord of the song—28—slowest of all) and naturally with the sustaining pedal.

Reprinted by permission of J. & W. Chester Ltd.

G DA1791 John McCormack (Gerald Moore)

MAILIED

Poem by GOETHE

Music by BEETHOVEN
Op. 52 No. 4

THE fact that Beethoven did not attain, in the lied, the glory of Schubert or the subtlety of Wolf is not sufficient reason for dismissing him as a song writer. So many of his songs—I say it in all humility—seem to be failures, that one concludes that this field was not his natural medium of expression. For all that, 'Adelaide', 'Wonne der Wehmuth', 'Die Ehre Gottes aus der Natur', 'In questa tomba oscura', and the cycle 'An die ferne geliebte', have, each in their own way, qualities of majesty or beauty or eloquence which make them great. They are alive today and they still stir us. I would not place 'Mailied' in the same category as the above, but I confess to an affection for it and am convinced that, handled in the right way, it is delightful.

I remember performing this song with Alexandra Trianti. We took it at a very fast *tempo*—the whole thing lasted only just over one and one-half minutes; a lot to cover in so short a time. Through its very speed it swept the audience off its feet and provoked enthusiasm, for its joy, redolent of the age of innocence, is infectious. Block harmony looks very pedestrian, but bars 19 to 22 for example skip along so lightly and are covered so quickly that the listener is quite unaware of the square-seeming chords in the accompaniment.

Ex. 1

wie glänzt die Son - ne, wie lacht die Flur !

'It sounds like a hymn tune' I was told, when listening to this passage being played too slowly and too substantially. But it must never sound like that: if it does then it is being played and sung in the wrong spirit.

Taken at speed the song is not easy to sing as the words have to be clear and only two breaths are taken in each of the first two verses. (In verse 1 a breath at 22 and 30, in verse 2 at bars 59 and 67.) If we adopt the Beethoven instruction *allegro*, if we count two beats to a bar, the music sinks back on its heels and the singer will have to breathe more frequently. Let us add the words '*con brio*' to the composer's *allegro* and carry through on our toes with one beat to a bar; bars 1 to 14 prior to the singer's entry will thus be played in one sweep; in a sweep, it is important to add, which embraces the singer who joins in to add impetus rather than to retard it. The bus does not slow down for the singer; she jumps on lightly and gracefully as it glides past her. I have drawn an arrow at 14, Ex. 2, to emphasize that there is no waiting on the pianist's part; the singer is impatient and if anything may come in a split second ahead of time. Good luck to her.

The singer is always *legato*, always smiling, but her enunciation is sharp so that 'wie lacht die Flur'—'o Erd, o Sonne, o Glück, o Lust' are really full of zest.

She makes us feel that it is good to be alive. This feeling is exemplified in the piano interlude, 38 to 51, to which the bird-like chirrups in the treble, and the sudden *fortes* and *pianos*, all contribute.

From 108, to help the singer maintain her buoyancy, the accompaniment literally bounces. It is all *staccato* and although it is *piano* and moves so quickly I try to raise my hands as high as possible between each chord. There is no time to lift the hands more than a few inches, but this, coupled with the fact that no sustaining pedal is used here, ensures that every chord is detached and electric.

I need hardly add that there is no *rallentando* whatsoever at the end of the song.

Published by Augener Ltd.

Sco 6oo8 Mme Decroix-Savoie
ALLO AL88 R. Herbert (F. Waldman)

WONNE DER WEHMUTH

Poem by GOETHE

Music by BEETHOVEN
Op. 83 No. 1

THE fate of 'Wonne der Wehmuth' depends on the answer to this question: will the soil, otherwise the singer's imagination, into which the precious seed of Beethoven's creation is dropped be fertile? I can listen to many a great piece of music performed in a routine, even a slipshod way, without a sense of personal outrage, because I love the music so dearly. An amateur orchestra, for instance, struggling with Schubert's 'Unfinished', playing slightly out of tune, with ragged attack, having no thought for the relation of one phrase to another but rather tackling each phrase as a separate obstacle fiercely to be overcome, will rouse in my breast a warm feeling of friendly sympathy but will not make me hate the symphony itself. This little gem of Beethoven's, however, stands or falls by the quality of its performance, and if it is indifferently sung or played one dislikes the very song itself. I myself did so, until I heard it sung, as it really should be sung, by the exquisite Elisabeth Schumann.

I regard *andante* as a misleading sign, for the *tempo* is slow, very slow; the first two bars take almost twenty seconds to cover and the performers would do well to take *largo* as a more fitting indication of the music's pace. The singer needs infinite poise. Although the mood is so emotional, her feelings are restrained, for the phrases which look so short on paper become quite long in actual execution and call for a sure command of the breath. The vocal line, despite all nuances, must be steady. 'Trocknet nicht' in bars 1 and 2—with no introduction to prepare us—is immediately expressive, and the thirty-second note on the second syllable of 'trocknet' is leisurely: one clearly hears the final consonant. These utterances together with the accompaniment's descent in the latter half of each bar are full of eloquence.

Ex. 1 *Andante espressivo*

I have indicated the points at which a slight increase and decrease of tone are desirable, but these signs are mine, they are not Beethoven's, and they should not be underlined; only suggested. So slight are these nuances that I hesitate to mention them but they should be felt, for these two bars are the kernel of the song, expressive and intense. The singer needs plenty of time for them and so does the accompanist, his descending scale being played with a *non legato* touch but with the pedal joining each note. He listens carefully to ensure that each note is less in quantity than the note before.

At bars 5 and 6 the piano echoes the singer's opening phrase, but it will jar the listener if the pianist, not quite certain in his mind how to shape the grace notes, accomplishes these turns clumsily. Counting four crotchets to each half bar, I have found the following the smoothest method:

Ex. 2

In the original, these turns are sixty-fourth notes (I have worked it out mathematically!), but each note is played so slowly that it is full of meaning. Please observe that the *crescendo* and *diminuendo* signs are Beethoven's.

Seeing the *sforzandi* in the accompaniment at 8 and 9 the singer should apply them particularly to the words 'Wie öde, wie todt die Welt ihm erscheint'.

But if the singer needed great breath control at 3 and 4, how much more taxing 14 and 15 will be. Many is the time I have heard the tone waver on the spot where the composer has written *ritard*; here too the singer is completely exposed without the cloak of an accompaniment to provide shelter.

Ex. 3

Bars 17, 18, 19 are the climax of the song. Here the singer seems to be staying an eternity on the G natural, yet the slow *tempo* must be maintained. It is very natural for an accompanist here to make a slight *accelerando* to help the inexpert singer over this formidable hurdle, and I am so much on the alert at this point to render what aid I can, that I found myself hastening these chords when rehearsing with Elizabeth Schwarzkopf. This consummate artist begged me, however, to keep inexorably to the slow *tempo* and the effect was glorious. What mastery from the singer it needs!

I have suggested by a comma at 18 after 'Thränen' where the singer may take a breath, and it is pretty certain most singers will need this breath if the *tempo* is slow enough.

Ex. 4

trock-net nicht, Thrä - nen un glück lich-er Lie - be!
17   18   19

As a postscript I should like to say a word about the beginning of this song. Since there is no pianoforte introduction it is an important preliminary to see that the singer knows the pitch of the note with which she starts; quite often the two partners have not discussed and have no clear understanding as to the way the accompanist should communicate it. To poke at it with the index finger is not to be recommended. The two most inoffensive means I know are to play a chord of E major—the chord to last an exact half bar in length or, carefully watching the singer, and *after* her breath has been taken, for the accompanist to play his chord a fraction of a second before the voice utters the note. The example below explains my meaning; but I must add that the chord is played extremely softly.

Ex. 5

Trock-net

If the singer has perfect pitch and needs no help, that is best of all, but it is not easy to find G sharp if the preceding song in your group was in a totally unrelated key.

Published by Augener Ltd.

G   DA1357   Elisabeth Schumann
T   A2781   Aullikki Rautawaara
ALLO AL88   R. Herbert (F. Waldman)

FELDEINSAMKEIT

Words by HERMANN ALMERS   *Music by* JOHANNES BRAHMS
                                                         Op. 86 No. 2

Ex.1 Langsam *(Slowly)*

Ich ru - he still im ho - hen grü-nen Gras und sen - de lan - ge mei - nen Blick nach o - ben nach

MOST of us, at some time or another, have had the experience of
lying in the grass, gazing upwards and feeling remote from the world

II

with only the cricket's chirrup in our ears and only the wide arch of sky to meet our eyes. The billowy clouds sailing across the blue had a mesmeric effect, so that while the body remained very much earth-bound the mind was caught up with the eyes into 'the limitless realms of the air'. 'Mir ist als ob ich längst gestorben bin'; it was an unearthly feeling, the soul seeming to have left the body. 'Feldeinsamkeit' awakens in us an echo of some such tranquil enjoyment as this.

In the right hand of the accompaniment the chords withdraw from earth's embrace and float up into the blue. The bass should always be played fairly solidly, not only as a reminder that we are earthbound, but because too ephemeral a tone will give insufficient support to the singer whose long *legato* phrases make this song a stern ordeal for him. Although the bass is substantial, the soft pedal is used all the time. No change of sustaining pedal is necessary for the first two bars, but thereafter, speaking generally, the pedal changes on the first and third beats.

Always the accompanist, watching the vocal line, gives the singer all the breathing space he needs. For instance, after 'lange' a breath may be wanted and time must be allowed for it. This gap in the vocal line can be covered up by the pianist joining the chord on 'lange' (5) to the chord on the first syllable of 'meinen' (6). If the accompanist on such an occasion as this 'breathes sympathetically' with the singer, it is most unsympathetic of him, for it draws attention to the singer's difficulty—allowing the listener to hear the machinery creaking. This is an instance which shows how necessary it is for performers to keep their secrets to themselves. By taking the audience into our confidence we disturb their repose, make them share the singer's trepidation, aware of the pianist's too obvious solicitude. Success for the singer lies in his ability to make his difficulties unapparent. Therefore when he breathes after 'lange' the singer will take a quiet and leisurely breath; a snatched breath would give the game away. He can only do this with the accompanist's help.

To sing contemplatively it is necessary to sing softly, one does not muse in a roaring *forte*; no *crescendo* should be made on the rising phrases of 3 and 4. After the breath at the end of bar 5, the singer feels like a giant refreshed, but he must restrain himself; listening carefully to himself he makes his first note of bar 6 exactly the same in volume as the preceding note.

The whole song is uniformly *piano* save where Brahms asks for a slight increase in tone. That arch at 'meinen Blick nach oben' is the more graceful by reason of its slenderness; any thickening of it by swelling the tone only coarsens it.

Six bars in each verse (12 to 17 in verse 1, 29 to 34 in verse 2) are notorious for their challenge to the singer.

Ex. 2

Undoubtedly the ideal way to sing these bars is with only one division for breath, at the comma after 'umwoben', bar 13, verse 1, and after 'Räume', bar 30, verse 2, though this may be found impossible at the slow *tempo* required. The singer who has not husbanded his resources during bars 12, 13, 14 will be in dire straits towards the end of 15, 16, 17; then will be heard the quavering tone, the struggle to sustain without support, the frenzied *accelerando* of the accompanist who realizes that his partner is going to keep his appointment on the first beat of 17 ahead of schedule. I have heard singers come such a cropper here that an expression of terror has appeared on their faces, a terror which grows during the second verse in anticipation of the next hurdle, 29 to 34, which is even more difficult to negotiate than its counterpart in verse 1. It is better to be safe than sorry, therefore I have indicated where it is best for breaths to be taken.

The semiquavers of the 'turn' in 16 and 33 should be as slow as possible, with plenty of time to 'look round' on the third beat, as if the world were standing still.

Ex. 3

No one who heard the incomparable Gerhardt do it will ever forget it.

The second verse is richer and even more exacting than the first. 'Die schönen weissen Wolken zieh'n dahin' ('white clouds floating gently above') is done in one sweep (at the corresponding bars in verse 1 we were able to take a breath) and so is 'wie schöne stille Träume' ('like lovely peaceful dreams'). By smoothness and continuity of vocal line the singer will do justice to the sudden B flat minor modulation with which Brahms has coloured the words.

Ex.4

Suspension of all movement is suggested here by the merest thread of tone. The *crescendo* is very slight and is there only to make it possible to effect the *diminuendo* in 24. *Mezza voce* prevails throughout the second verse.

'I feel as though I were dead' is the crux of the song and should be delivered without expression: warmth of tone or a point-making of 'gestorben' will rob the phrase of its unearthliness.

Ex.5

It is unearthly but not morbid, and the fact that Brahms handles the situation above in the same way that he treats it in the second of the Four Serious Songs Opus 121 No. 2, should not confuse the performers.

Ex. 6

From Brahms. *Vier ernste gesänge*

Da lob te ich die Tod - ten
Then I did praise the dead.

You see in both examples the voice descending and the detached stepping-down octaves in the accompaniment; you see Brahms in each case inclining his head. But whereas the excerpt from the Four Serious Songs is imbued with religious awe, the crucial phrase in Example 5 must be sung with serene wonderment, for the sensation is one of elation, of a floating de-materialization: there is no movement, there is only space and emptiness. To preserve this the pianist should resist a tendency to hasten at bar 28. Nothing seems to be happening in this bar, and that is how it should be.

Hermann Almers and Johannes Brahms have given us a deeply felt song which cannot be sung too slowly. It should take at least four minutes to perform.

Published by N. Simrock

G	D2009	Elena Gerhardt
C	7204M	Alexander Kipnis (Gerald Moore)
PD	30009	Heinrich Schlusnus (Franz Rupp)
G	EW9	Julia Culp (Fritz Lindemann)
G	EG3308	Gerhard Hüsch (Hans Udo Müller)
PD	19977	Leo Slezak
G	E328	Leopold Demuth
C	LX1403	Hans Hotter (Gerald Moore)
G	DA635	John McCormack (Edwin Schneider)
Voc	A0216	Elena Gerhardt (Ivor Newton)
PD	B22169	Leo Slezak
D	K1665	Paul Schoeffler (Ernest Lush)
T	A2040	Karl Schmitt-Walter (Franz Rupp)
V	10-1405	Lotte Lehmann (Paul Ulanowsky)
G	DB3285	Maria Müller (Ivor Newton)
West	WL5053	A. Poell (V. Graef)
P	PE128	P. Munteanu (G. Favaretto)

MEINE LIEBE IST GRÜN

Poem by FELIX SCHUMANN

Music by JOHANNES BRAHMS
Op. 63 No. 5

'MEINE Liebe ist grün' refutes Wolf's criticism that Brahms 'could not exult'. It is true that the mood of unrestrained happiness did not come easily to him. Sometimes he laboured in vain for it, as in the heavy-footed 'O liebliche Wangen', which his critics are quick to seize on in substantiation of their charge.

But the composer's misses are surely outweighed by the bull's-eyes he has scored in such songs as 'Der Gang zum Liebchen', Opus 48 No. 1; 'Auf dem Schiffe', Opus 97 No. 2; 'Frühlingstrost', Opus 63 No. 1; and 'O komme holde Sommernacht', Opus 58 No. 4.

'Meine Liebe ist grün' is a paean of joy from beginning to end, and those who have not found it so cannot have heard Gerhardt, Lehmann, John Coates, and Kipnis sing it. The vocal line does indeed seem to give the singer the 'wings of a nightingale' as it sweeps higher and higher.

Ex. 1 *With animation*

Mei ne Lie - be ist grün

wie der Flie - der busch, und mein

The song must start with a burst from the very first note. It does not gradually get into its stride, it shoots off like a rocket. Singer and

16

pianist will be able to get together if a preliminary chord is played (like a precautionary 'Are you ready?') before beginning the song. This ensures a fair start.

The singer must make the most of his flights on to the higher notes. The spacing of the notes in bars 1 and 2 allows for this; but the final quavers of bar 7 can be slightly stressed. The marks on these notes are my own. By hurrying the reiterated D naturals and final quavers of bars 9 and 11 slightly, we are able to spend a little more time on the top, in bars 10 and 12, while the final climax in bar 14 (G sharp and F sharp) is quite spacious, with the *tempo* resumed in bar 15.

Ex. 2

The song takes little more than a minute to perform and it is unnecessary to attempt any contrast in the treatment of the two verses. They are musically the same. Bars 1 to 16 should be treated as one line; the rests should not be regarded as punctuations, giving the feeling of a succession of small phrases, Brahms very kindly put them there to enable the singer to take in air. Snatched breaths are all the singer will have time for, and if he feels he is hardly done by let him remember that he is suffering in a good cause, for the impression he seeks to create is one of breathless joy. I think Brahms must have had this in mind by the wide drop of a sixth in bars 15 and 35, which suggests not the evaporation of enthusiasm—but breathlessness.

The performance of this song is frequently spoiled by the pianist. He gets in the way of the singer. The latter has a clean line, while the accompanist admittedly has a mass of notes to contain, with some awkward leaps into the bargain. The success or failure of 'Meine Liebe ist grün' depends very largely on the pianist, whose playing above all wants vitality. But this does not necessarily mean that he gives an equally weighted *forte* on every note of the song, though a glance at the first three bars of Example 1 might suggest this. The following markings (my own) will give an idea how the passages in the left hand should be tackled (Example 3).

In the first two bars a kick is wanted on the low bass notes, and a burst on to the top D sharp and on to the C sharps in bar 3. A diminution of tone is made in the descent of the *arpeggiando* to make the booms of the bass notes and the bursts on the top notes stand out more clearly, but the general level of tone being *forte* this is not to be overdone.

Ex. 3

At the singer's big sweeps on bars 9, 10, and 11, 12 the accompaniment is phrased to correspond with the vocal urge to the top notes on 'Flieder-busch' and 'Wonne', while the bass octaves in bars 13, 14 must be huge. But what of the right hand? It is turning on the heat, supplying the impetuosity. It syncopates throughout the whole song as shown in Example 1. While the singer takes his breath at bar 4 and most especially on his high notes in bars 10, 12, 14 the pianist clatters.

I hope it will not be thought that in Example 3 and my recommendations following, I am showing how I can improve on Brahms. I am only trying to indicate how a pianist can match the singer's enthusiasm and be of immense support to him in this strenuous song. The singer will not feel he is waging a lone battle against hopeless odds.

In one place—and in one place only—do I deliberately contravene Brahms's instruction, this is bars 19, 20, and of course the corresponding bars 39, 40: it is when the piano is solo.

Ex. 4

The above are Brahms's markings and I quarrel with the *fermata* on the first beat of bar 20. Played thus it seems to me that the lively *tempo* (resumed on the second quaver of the bar) gets off to a very dusty start. I prefer to make my *fermata* on the fourth beat of 19 waiting as long as I like—and then starting the quick *tempo* on the first beat of bar 20, as follows:

The accent (*piano*) coming on the first beat of the bar draws the loose reins together and off we gallop again.

I may be completely mistaken in my notion of the above but I have played it for hundreds of singers and they have never been at odds with me over this passage. In any case whether the student agrees or disagrees with me he must see that there is no flagging in the 'symphony' after each verse, it should quicken right up to the *fermata*.

The last two bars of the song should be played in strict time.

Max Friedlander, in his admirable book *Brahms's Lieder* (O.U.P.) says of these bars 'one can not say whether the effect of the piano signifies a faint anxiety, hesitation and doubt, or peaceful calm', but I think this is reading too much into it. The penultimate bar pants with physical fatigue. The last chord is, speaking metaphorically, like a grunt of satisfaction as one drops exhausted into an armchair. Not a bad idea for the singer and pianist who have performed the song properly.

The poem, in case one hears a stray word from time to time, is by Felix Schumann, son of Robert and Clara and godson of Brahms.

Published by Peters

G	DA1469	Lotte Lehmann (Erno Balogh)
PD	25014	Julius Patzak (Franz Rupp)
G	DA1586	Kirsten Flagstad (Edwin MacArthur)
V	17746	Alexander Kipnis (Ernst Wolff)
D	LX3051	Suzanne Danco (G. Agosti)

VERGEBLICHES STÄNDCHEN

(Niederrheinisches Volkslied)　　　　　Music by JOHANNES BRAHMS
Op. 84 No. 4

I THINK we can picture the youth in this song as a country bumpkin not over-burdened with wit, for how else can his uncouth wooing be explained? Indeed it is hard to resist the suspicion that though his day may have been spent harmlessly enough in pushing the plough, our rustic serenader has spent the evening in the local tavern. Let us put it this way, he is very, very happy—'Gut gelaunt' as Brahms has it. In this spirit he calls up to the window of his sweetheart not in a pleading whisper, melting to the hardest heart, but with a full-throated confident bawl whose effect speedily brings the girl to her window and which threatens to rouse the entire neighbourhood. The girl's mother, we gather, seems to hold some prejudice against young men interviewing young ladies late at night, and it is long past bedtime; it is five minutes past ten. Mamma, that vigilant guardian, sleeps with one eye open.

Rolling down the lane on his heels and singing lustily comes our young hopeful:

Ex. 1 *Lebhaft, gut gelaunt*

Gu-ten A - bend mein Schatz, gu-ten A - bend mein kind,

The treatment of this verse should be hale and hearty. Despite its jocosity it gives such an impression of rough masculinity that we are surprised in the second verse—where the girl sings—how graceful and light-footed the same music can sound. If the *piano* and *pianissimo* signs in Verse 1 are ignored, Verse 2 being all *piano* will provide a far greater contrast, and this is the way I like it.

Foreshadowing the appearance of the girl at her window, the accompanist at bar 20, making no *crescendo*, plays softly and daintily, changing character with the singer.

Like all pretty young women, the heroine of our story holds the whip hand; her summing up and handling of the situation is masterly. With sound tactical sense—one would almost call it generalship—she brushes aside the jovial salutation and the declaration 'Ich komm'aus Lieb' zu dir', and concerns herself solely with the plea 'Open your door to me' which she considers as being of more pressing importance.

Replying with commendable forthrightness she answers, 'My door is locked, I'll not let you in', and adds as a *coup de grâce*, 'Mother has given me very good advice about such goings on.'

In spite of this rude awakening from slumber the young girl is not in an ill-humour but rather enjoys making the fellow look stupid. This verse therefore should be sung with the lightness of touch befitting one whose words are not intended to be overheard by all and sundry, yet it should be delivered with that relish invariably enjoyed by the female when punishing the delinquent male.

But come, the boy is not so stupid after all, or can it be that the cold night air has had a sobering effect? At all events he tries a new dodge in the third verse. He pleads 'It's so cold out here and the wind is like ice—do let me in.'

Ex. 2

The pianist plays an important part here, for he supplies the icy blast and shows the shivering figure. By holding the sustaining pedal at bars 43, 44, 45, and at 47, 48 (and of course maintaining the *forte*) an effect of howling wind can be obtained; while the accents on the second beat of 52 and 54 (Example 3) are indicative of a cold shiver, the *staccato* chords contributing to this impression.

At bar 60 the dismissal of the village Romeo is signalled by an *animato* sign leading to 'You go home to bed. Goodnight, my lad.' Again I recommend the abrogation of the *forte* at 61, for the singer and pianist must use a light tone all through the girl's verse. The *leggiero*

Ex. 3

sign at 71 is of special significance in that it enables us to appreciate that behind the apparent severity of her remarks the girl can hardly conceal her amusement. It is sung with a smile to an accompaniment which almost titters and which I like played with more *staccato* than is marked.

Ex. 4

There are several ways of singing bars 75 to 80, my preference is as follows:

Ex. 5

The slackened speed in 75 and the slight *tenuto* are coquettish, while the resumption of *tempo* at 77 is peremptory and not without humour. A *rallentando* which some people like, from 77 to the end, is too pedestrian.

Surely Brahms is telling us by the *sforzando* in 82 that the girl is closing her window with a slam.

Ex. 6

At all events, that is my reading of it, and this accounts for the bad language in 83, 84 which the thwarted youth might well use. I ought to explain to the reader, who might take me too literally, that I do not utter these words aloud when playing these chords at the end of the postlude—they only pass through my mind.

Max Friedlander tells us that Brahms desired a serious interpretation for 'Vergebliches Ständchen' but I cannot see it at all in this light. Brahms's own instructions are 'With animation and good humour' and that is the way it should be. The song ought to raise a smile.

Published by Peters

G	DA1417	Elisabeth Schumann (George Reeves)
G	D2007	Elena Gerhardt
G	(Soc)	Alexander Kipnis (Gerald Moore)
P	R020530	Richard Tauber (Percy Kahn)
Voc	B3115	Elena Gerhardt
P	R020159	Lotte Lehmann
Pat	X93116	Lucien Muratore

VON EWIGER LIEBE

Poem by WENTZIG   *Music by* JOHANNES BRAHMS
Op. 43 No. 1

DARKNESS has fallen over woodland and field; it is evening and the world is still. No light is seen, nor smoke from chimney, and the lark no longer sings. A lad comes from the village seeing his sweetheart home, he takes her by the willow wood talking earnestly. 'If you are distressed and ashamed because of me, the bond of our love will be severed as swiftly as it was tied and we will part as quickly as we were united.' The maiden replies: 'Our bond of love will never be severed! Steel and iron are strong, but our love is stronger! Iron and steel can be forged but how can our love be changed? Iron and steel can be melted but our love will last for ever!'

'Von Ewiger Liebe' is a big song and it must be performed in a big way. It is an oil painting on a large canvas in which essential clarity of detail does not obscure the whole. Detailed effect in this phrase and that, after being practised and mastered, are then regarded as subsidiary; the wood can be seen in spite of the trees. Although there is a rising phrase here, a falling phrase there, now a big *crescendo*, now an *accelerando*—all these become subservient to the overall uphill dynamic climb culminating in the grand climax which is not reached until the very end of the song, bars 113 to 117, 'unsere Liebe muss ewig bestehn'.

'Good,' says the student, 'then arrangements must be made accordingly. I will conserve my energy until I reach this point and on the road towards it I will sing *mezzoforte* where a *forte* is marked, I will sing *piano* for a *mezzoforte*, a *pianissimo* for a *piano*; then when I come to the climax I will let them have it. I will thunder.' But this artful dodge will not do. One's mind must, of course, from the very first be aware of the goal, of the supreme point waiting so far ahead, but the song will surely be emasculated by this process of planing down the dynamics. 'Our love is stronger than iron and steel,' declares the maiden: singer and pianist have this at the back of their minds before they embark on this song, for it is a song of strength and purpose and conviction. Not finesse, which implies artificiality, nor craft implying cunning, are demanded from the performers but rather, sincerity and a good heart; in one word—honesty. The miniaturist should fight shy of this song for it needs a Kathleen Ferrier, with a Kathleen Ferrier's nobility of spirit and glory of voice.

There are so many varieties of tone and colour in which singer and

24

pianist can indulge, *piano* or *pianissimo*, *forte* or *mezzoforte*, that it is impossible to find enough labels to tag on to them. Weight and quality of tone cannot be categorized. The *forte* or *fortissimo*, for instance, in a Chopin Nocturne is quite different in value from that in a Chopin Scherzo. In the latter the *forte* may need percussive brilliance and dash, while the Nocturne's *forte* is only a comparative one, only a swelling of tone in a *cantabile* passage. The *piano* mark for instance at the opening of 'Von Ewiger Liebe' is quite different in meaning from the *piano* mark in Brahms's 'Wiegenlied': one is sombre and heavy, arresting the attention; the other lulls us.

With the implication of the words of the first verse in his mind the pianist's four-bar introduction is played with a firm *legato* touch, the bass notes predominating. A certain intensity of feeling can mark this introduction, it is portentous, but at bar 4 the pianist can relax a little (in other words make a *diminuendo*) for the opening verse is purely descriptive ('Not a movement is to be seen nor a sound heard as night sinks over village and field'), and calls for a dark but unemotional quality of tone. Bars 5 to 12 should be sung in two curves, 5 to 8 the upward curve, 9 to 12 the downward. They are majestic phrases but lose in dignity if divided thus: 5–6 up, 7–8 down, 9–10 up, 11–12 down. Brahms himself has marked bars 14 to 21 with these big curves by *crescendo* and *diminuendo* signs and the singer should give the same shape to his earlier phrases.

Ex. 1

The phrase marks are mine. I have inserted them, as I have the *crescendo* and *diminuendo* signs, to indicate how the singer should think of the long line. Certainly a breath can be quietly taken on the quaver rest in bar 6 though a breath in bar 5 is hardly needed—albeit the quaver rest should be observed: the comma after 'es', bar 10, enables another breath to be taken if wanted.

I give Brahms's marking for bars 14 to 21 which plainly show that my treatment of Example 1 is not too far removed from the composer's idea.

Ex. 2

A breath can be permitted after 'Licht' but 'Rauch ja' should be joined.

A sense of restlessness, which is inherent in the music, can only be parried by the performers' determination to avoid over-emotionalizing and by maintaining long smooth lines. Movement comes in the second verse ('a lad escorting his sweetheart emerges from the village') and can be conveyed by a casting off of the restraint exercised in verse 1 and an increase of the tone to a *mezzopiano*; all this anticipated by the accompanist (bars 21 to 24). A quickening of *tempo* is inadvisable, for it will nullify the effect of a *stringendo* which is to come much later. Small though the difference may be between verses 1 and 2 in the musical text, it is an important one. It lies in the altered dynamics at the end of the verse. Bars 18 to 21 droop away but 38 to 41 surge upwards threateningly—the voice, on the last syllable of 'mancherlei', keeping to the F sharp—a reiterated note which heightens the lovers' tension.

Ex. 3

This verse, ending as it does in the middle of a sentence ('earnestly the lad said—'), the three-bar gap has to be bridged by the singer's thought which carries the listener along with him. This thought is sustained only by the pianist's playing. Everything depends on the pianist. His four bars (41 to 44) are note for note the same as his introduction to the first and second verses (1 to 4 and 21 to 24), but this time, picturing the lad's white-faced protestation, he plays them with white-hot intensity, he presses down each note knowing that he is carrying the song by the urgency of his playing.

Ex. 4

To fulfil the demands made above, a good *mezzoforte* is sufficient. Feeling, not loudness, gives intensity to the tone.

Pain and heartache underlie the lad's passionate declaration that he will part from his love rather than cause her suffering; these are symbolized by the cross rhythm between the vocal quavers and the triplets in the accompaniment. The twos against the threes must be steady and strong. Like blocks of granite the music piles up now in sections; 45 to 52 is overtopped by the *poco piu forte e poco stringendo*. Each section is but a part of one chapter and the links to each section are strung by the pianist's climbing and loudening triplets in bars 52 and 60. These links are played with terrible intensity, for by them the singer is stimulated to heighten the volume of sound.

Ex. 5

Arriving at bar 61 another organ stop is pulled out—the *tempo* quickens and works up to the passionate—

Ex. 6

Schnell wie wir frü - her ver - ei - ni - get sind."

Turbulent though the music has been from bar 45 to 72 the pinnacle of the song has not yet been attained: the performers still hold some power in reserve: boiling-point was almost reached, but not quite. Yet the listener must not be aware of this; to him the piling up of these blocks of sound has culminated in a huge climax of breath-taking intensity. Singer and pianist do not arouse suspicion by 'pulling their punches'—to use a boxing metaphor—for this would be insincere and quite unconvincing. They must put tremendous energy and power into it without driving themselves to the utmost limit of their capacity.

A *forte* is marked at bar 68, but it wants a *fortissimo*. The left hand thunders and is heard over and above the accompanying and insistent right-hand triplets. A *non legato* clatter is easily achieved but should be avoided even at the cost of a slight smudging of harmonies as I have indicated by my pedalling. From bar 72 the long line descends into (I stress the word 'into') the 'Ziemlich langsam' section, bar 79.

Ex.7

The slow section must be joined dynamically and rhythmically to the preceding bars. Judgement is needed to achieve this. First of all the accompanist sees that his tone, decreasing in volume as the music descends, is a gradual reduction so that at bar 78 he is already anticipating the *pianissimo* quality of the next bar: also he must arrange his *ritardando* so that his right hand quavers, slowing up by degrees, actually establish the 6/8 rhythm of bar 79 with the last triplet of 78. Thus the two sections are dovetailed. A perfect fusion is essential to hold the song together, for the section we are now approaching bears no musical relation whatsoever to the last—unless indeed we look on the song as an emotional cadence—the boy's utterance being the unsatisfied discord, the girl's the serene transcendental tonic. For certainly, the fervid turbulence of the boy resolves itself into the sublime faith of the girl; a faith which expresses itself in music of spacious dignity and nobility. We sense the presence of a character so much stronger than the lad's, notwithstanding his passionate protestations. He does well to worship her and fall at her feet when she declares 'Our love is stronger than iron or steel—our love is eternal.' We are lifted to a higher plane and it is for this that the singer has been husbanding her resources; it was of this that singer and accompanist were thinking at the commencement of the song. Appropriately enough this calm strength is introduced by the quietest means, the voice part moving in long steady lines to the accompaniment of an undulating, unagitating figure in the pianoforte (as seen in bar 79, Example 7).

Ex. 8

No sign of the 'Sturm und drang' through which she passed is seen on the singer's face or heard in her voice. Bars 83 to 86 are taken in one breath; snatch a breath after 'Liebe' and the phrase founders, the meaning goes out of the words. The grace notes in bar 85 (and 105) should be treated as ordinary semiquavers, unhurried, as follows:

Ex. 8a

Now the music gains momentum and works up to a *forte* ('unsere Liebe ist fester noch mehr'). It is a foothill of the high peak towards which we are working. The accompaniment leaps and surges in waves under the upward curve of the voice (86 to 94) then ebbs quietly away in a *ritardando* to a *dolce* in preparation for the long final climb. Once again the pianist links these two sections together. The *tempo* at 94 is quicker after the *animato* sign at 88, and the *diminuendo* and *ritardando* in the pianoforte merge gradually into the rather slow time again, re-establishing at 99 the *tempo* we used at 79.

Ex. 9

Brahms's instruction at 93 and 94 is *mezzoforte*, but this is not enough; it needs a good big *forte*. Strict observance of the *dolce* at 99 is necessary, this gives the singer all the space she needs to make the huge *crescendo* which takes us up to the peak:

Ex. 10

Both the *fortissimo* marks at 113 and 117 are mine; Brahms has only marked *forte* which is quite inadequate. This grand and sustained climax needs all the power the singer has and all the support that the pianist can press into his keys. A breath is taken before the final 'ewig'.

At 113 and 114 the piano has a definite 3/4 rhythm clearly marked in the grouping of the right-hand quavers and in the three beats, each strongly emphasized, in the bass. Against this the voice sails on undisturbed and triumphant. It is the great moment of the song and as such it deserves 'lebensraum': in other words it wants space. The *animato* which has prevailed since 108 must give way to a broader slower *tempo* at 113—and the last 'ewig' is given as much time as the singer wants to spend on it, consistent with the quaver movement in the accompaniment, on which the pianist makes a *molto rallentando*. Actually the singer feels the beats of the slowing quavers underneath her and will be guided by them so that she can meet the accompanist on the second syllable of 'ewig'. It is very inconsiderate of a singer and a sign of bad musicianship if, after her partner's well-executed *molto rallentando* (i.e. a lengthening in ever-increasing proportions of the six quavers), she hangs the accompanist up for an eternity on the last quaver before coming down on the second syllable.

From 117 (seen above) the pianoforte finishes off the song, making a *ritardando* as Brahms instructs.

I cannot help feeling that the *piano* sign in 121 can easily be mis-understood: the tone should indeed be less in volume than it was at the crowning moment of the vocal arch (115–116), but it should not become too attenuated. A rich and healthy chord, but not a violent one, is much to be preferred; indeed to ensure this I plead guilty to em-bellishing the final chord in the following manner after having given stress on the preceding quaver.

'Von ewiger Liebe' ends in a blaze of glory.

Published by Peters

G	DB1021	Elena Gerhardt
G	DB1485	Sigrid Onegin
PD	95468	Maria Olszewska
G	DB1937	Dusolina Giannini
P	Er1100	Emmy Bettendorf
G	DB2994	Alexander Kipnis (Gerald Moore)
PD	67538	Heinrich Schlusnus (Sebastian Peschko)
G	DB5540	Tiana Lemnitz (Bruno Seidler-Winkler)
PD	B22432	Herman Jadlowker
G	DB21457	Victoria de los Angeles (Gerald Moore)
PD	68299	Margarete Klose
P	R20013	Lotte Lehmann

LOVELIEST OF TREES

Words by A. E. HOUSMAN *Music by* GEORGE BUTTERWORTH

GEORGE BERNARD SHAW has said that many of his plays are actor-proof. He meant that his own creation was so wonderful in itself—he admitted it—that no bad acting could mar it. Whether such a dictum could be applied to a musical composition is extremely arguable. Perhaps Caccini's 'Amarylli' or Handel's 'Ombra mai fu', given a lovely tone and a lawful regard for note values, can survive a lack of personality or the highest quality of musicianship from the performer: perhaps the music here speaks for itself without any help from the 'interpreter'. I do not subscribe to this view entirely though it embodies a warning which performers cannot afford to ignore. It is the easiest thing in the world for the singer, for the accompanist, to get in the way, to come between the song and the audience.

But at least let us give credit to the taste of the artists who know when to leave well alone, for it is certain that the choice (when to do—when not to do) is in the hands of the performer. Here, the smouldering fire is left alone and there we fan it into flames.

We resent having the virtuoso conductor's signature scrawled all over what he calls 'My Beethoven', yet we welcome the personality, the passionate lyricism that a Beecham puts into Delius.

To say that 'Loveliest of Trees' is a song needing all the poetry, musicianship, and personal assertion that a singer can pour into it, is not to minimize the genius of Butterworth. He never wrote two notes where one note would do; not an ounce of superfluous fat do you find in his music. He paid the singer and the accompanist the compliment of marking on his score '*Sempre rubato e con espressione*', saying in effect, 'I leave it to you. Shape, give curve and elasticity to my phrase; breathe life and passion into it.'

Ex. 1

33

Butterworth's economy of notes is evident in this example. The singer, seeing it for the first time, might consider that the vocal line is given a very bare accompaniment. If his partner, however, shares with him the rapture that the words and eventually the music inspire, he will find that the piano part is full of colour and meaning. Bars 1 to 3 are buoyant and pliable; they are not played strictly in time. Here is a situation where the accompanist does not 'establish a *tempo*', his introduction is *quasi recitative*: bar 1 is long; bar 2 is long, yet in spite of my stresses, the quavers gather speed as they lessen in weight, making 3 a short bar. The singer, as I have shown by the arrow, enters as soon as he hears the F sharp in the bass, but once in, he lingers; he must feel free to take 4 and 5 as spaciously as he pleases, it would be a pity to hasten the C sharp on the second syllable of 'loveliest'. Only on the last beat of 5 does he indicate the basic *tempo* of the song; he settles this *tempo* in 6 and 7. At 8 the quavers in the accompaniment shape the *ritenuto*; while the first quaver group is *legato*, the second (*pp*) is detached but with sustaining pedal. The effect is of a gleaming softness—you can see the glancing light on the bloom.

From 9 until 29 the *tempo* is maintained (except at 11–12 where the accompaniment repeats the figure of 1–2 and with the same freedom). 'Wearing white for Eastertide' is glorious; the singer puts all his warmth into it as the music surges forward.

'White' on its high note can easily be made to glow, but 'Eastertide' gives the singer a problem, for the volume is greater than at 'white'.

Wear - ing white ___ for East - er - tide. ___
13   14   15   16

When he embarks on his *crescendo* at 13 he should remember what
is required of him at 16. And at 16 the accompanist must not be
merciful, he started loudening with his partner, but he goes further still
to a very big climax at 18. If he discreetly lessens his tone so as not to
cover the voice the march of the great *crescendo* will be interrupted. The
climax with Butterworth's markings is wrung from the piano.

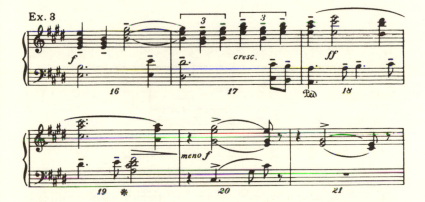

The singer exults while these white banners for Easter are waving; only
at 20 and 21 where the piano sounds a warning do his thoughts give
him pause.

Now, of my three - score years and ten,
22   23   24

Twen - ty will not come a - gain,
25   26

These misgivings are eloquently echoed in the piano part.

As I have said the *tempo* is maintained all the time. Indeed as it
dawns on the singer that there are only fifty springs left for him to enjoy,
the pace is inclined to quicken: this is at 27.

If we have slightly accelerated in that ascending passage we pay back the time borrowed at 30, 31 where the singer's *poco ritardando* is continued in the piano part. ('Ah, yes' the accompaniment sadly agrees.)

Finally after a three-bar *crescendo* comes the resolution to which the poet and composer have been leading us. The singer seems to clasp the woodlands, the blossoms, the world to his breast.

This is the crux of the song. The *largamente* gives us time to turn round and survey the scene and gives us time for a spiritual and vocal expansion. Perfect understanding is necessary between singer and accom-

see the cher - ry hung with snow.

panist, the latter can incommode his partner very easily as it is he who shapes the course of this *largamente*. Thick and heavy the quaver accompaniment must be, yet it is supple, ready to move forward at 40, 41, 42 preparatory to its joyous flight in 43. Yes, 43 is all joy.

Ex. 7

Let us sing on the piano with all our soul, making the most of it while we may, for we are gently reminded (44, 45) that life is short, spring is fleeting.

D AM506   Roy Henderson (Gerald Moore)

EN SOURDINE

Words by PAUL VERLAINE   *Music by* CLAUDE DEBUSSY

IT is always fascinating and instructive to compare various musical settings of the same poem. As I shall illustrate later in this book, in John
Fletcher's poem 'Sleep' Ivor Gurney finds tortured restlessness where
Peter Warlock finds infinite repose: Schumann tosses 'Wenn durch die
Piazzetta' up in the air and catches it again with a laugh, but Mendelssohn lays his hand on his heart in earnest protestation. Again, the two
settings of 'Die ihr schwebet um diese Palmen' by Brahms and by Wolf
provide us with an equally great contrast. Brahms sets the words to the
tune of an old lullaby, 'Josef, lieber Josef mein', where the Babe is
rocked to sleep in the arms of the Virgin Mary, but Hugo Wolf is much
more concerned with the angry rustling and swaying of the palm-trees,
fearful that their noise will awaken the sleeping child. We should seize
avidly on such contrasts for they give us an illumination into the mind
and heart of the composer, and it is by comparing them that we find
that where one composer gives precedence to a certain train of the
poet's thought (not necessarily by forcing it on our attention with
vehemence but perhaps by putting his finger to his lips to enjoin
secrecy) the other subordinates this very same thought and gives pro-
minence to an entirely different poetic idea.

These thoughts came to me while studying Debussy's 'En Sourdine'
side by side with Fauré's. The last line of this exquisite little poem of
Verlaine's ('Voix de notre desespoir, le rossignol chantera') dominates
Debussy's mind, he gives us the song of the nightingale in the very first
bar of the accompaniment and persists with it almost throughout,
letting the voice act as an *obligato*.

Ex. 1   *Rêveusement lent*   Debussy

pp *Doux et expressif*

Singing dreamily, the lover hears the bird calling insistently (in the piano part).

The stresses give point to the words but do not lessen the extreme languor of the mood, a languor which becomes patent to us when we compare it with Fauré's fullness of heart, in Example 2.

This poignancy, not discounted by the composer's *dolce* recommendation, is still further heightened by the whispered intimacy, the underlying passion decorously unfolded, of Example 3.

In this passage is enshrined the tender, quivering, reverential passion of Fauré: but these particular lines do not affect Debussy in the same way.

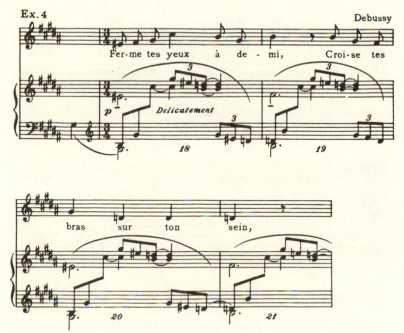

Here we see a lover, truly a tender lover, but one who is sure his invocation will not be in vain: the softly moving accompaniment is a delicate caress.

From 18 to 31 Debussy's nightingale is silent, but it is a felicitous section, with the soft rustle of the grasses and leaves stealing on the ear in the accompaniment.

Such a mood is too tranquil to be disturbed save by the gentle plaint of the nightingale, to which the singer finally alludes in a phrase that haunts the listener long after the song is ended.

Ravishing! At last after its lengthy meditative undertone, occasionally seeming to have been submerged by the pianoforte, the voice rises high above the accompaniment. It is still *sotto voce*, but Debussy has thrown it up prominently, made it his emotional climax. But Fauré's climax is elsewhere; he is most sonorous at 'Et quand, solennel, le soir des chênes noirs tombera', with an ample curve for the singer and a portentous organ-like accompaniment.

Both songs need the most delicate approach; in the Debussy, uncouth or careless playing by the accompanist will goad a singer into raising his voice beyond the dreamy calm the composer wants. The singer on the other hand who uses too much tone makes it incumbent on the pianist to make his song a strident one: if both partners are quiet and reserved, and each listens to the other, their two voices will be clearly heard.

In the middle section, 18 to 31, the singer is a little less subdued but takes care that his line is smooth, and the pianist merely brushes the keys. Concentrated practice is needed at 29 and 30 where the grace of the transitional passage will be squandered unless the intonation is perfect: the notes must be picked out with affectionate nicety while still preserving the *legato*.

Ex. 7

By judicious pedalling the accompanist will match his partner's smoothness. In Example 6 the voice is poised with limpid purity, and we listen greedily for the nostalgic chords on the last syllables of 'desespoir' and 'chantera'.

As I suggested earlier, a study of Fauré's song will give the student a clearer light on Debussy's in spite of, or because of the vast difference between the two settings. If I admit to a preference for the former, it is not to say that I decry the latter, for the Debussy song is lovely to hear, to sing, and to play, and is indeed a magical setting of the words. It is not so deeply felt as the other, but it enchants us.

Reprinted by permission of Messrs. J. Jobert, Paris (Fauré's 'En Sourdine' published by J. Hamelle & Co., Paris)

G   DA1471   Maggie Teyte (Gerald Moore)
IRCC 35   Nellie Melba

LES CLOCHES

Poem by PAUL BOURGET   *Music by* CLAUDE DEBUSSY

THE church bells calling from afar as we stand in the woodlands strike a nostalgic chord in our hearts and bring to mind absent friends and times past.

Let us not forget that the chimes are heard in the distance; perhaps their spell would be broken, our ears deafened by their noisy clangour were we too near them. Can it be that distance lends enchantment?

This song is softly sung and played. Through it all unceasingly and with unchanging tonality runs the little theme of the bells (C sharp, D sharp, E—as seen in every example where I give the accompaniment). This chime must be heard all the time for it inspires the singer's thoughts and is the thread on which the vocal line is embroidered. The singer wants to feel this accompanying chime through his singing, and will only do so if he himself observes the *piano* and *doux* signs which are there in plenty, for by singing too heavily he will impel the accompanist's tone to be increased proportionately—the 'lointain appel' thus becoming quite meaningless. Once only is the singer asked to raise his voice to a *mezzoforte*. Accompanists too are reminded that the singer listening to distant chimes is in the woodland, the first words being 'On the branches the leaves are opening—delicately.' The gently rustling branches are in the right-hand figure.

45

As befits a soliloquy the song should be sung with the smoothest *legato* line; in the example above, no breath is taken until after 'branches'. Only the four quavers of 'delicatement', bar 5, are the exception to the uniform *legato*—they are not *staccato*, they are merely *non legato*; little pin-points of light which become almost too material if treated in *legato* style. It is the easiest thing in the world to distort the triplet in bar 4— to make it

and many singers do this, for it is following the line of least resistance by fitting so comfortably with the quavers in the piano part; but the effect of the three against the four carries the thought of the singer so much more effectively that Debussy uses it seven times in the song.

Provided his right hand is lightly used, the pianist can use his sustaining pedal as I have indicated. In an impressionist picture of this nature the colours can be blurred a little and an effect of mingled chimes is created. When the bell figure is harmonized from bar 7 onwards, however, the pedal is used with more discrimination.

The C sharp on the first beat of bar 10 can be taken with the right hand to avoid spreading the chord. Always the bell's call predominates; the lower harmonies in the bass and the right-hand figure stay in the background.

'This distant call' says the singer,

and Debussy knows that we shall have made a *crescendo* on the rising phrase (bars 16 and 17) culminating in the triplet figure (it is not marked but it is natural and quite in order to make it), so he wisely writes a *diminuendo* on bar 19; for 'Des fleurs de l'autel' is sung reverentially. Not perhaps since his childhood—certainly not for years—has the soliloquizer had this picture of the white flowers on the church's altar brought back to him so vividly, a picture which is still capable of awakening the awe of earlier days. He silently muses, listening to the bells' more insistent pealing.

Ex. 4

Bars 21 to 24 must be played with more urgency for they affect the singer's next utterance; he draws on them to feed his growing emotion. The pianist can obtain this urgency not only by giving added stress to the chime (now heard high up in the treble) but by a surge of tone on the quavers where the *crescendo* is marked. I find that I do not get slower in this section although Debussy's instruction is unmistakable, indeed I have to resist a temptation to go faster, such is my anxiety to express a quickened emotion. But I obtain this, I hope, by tense touch rather than by increased speed. 'Those chimes,' says the singer, 'speak to me of happy years gone by'—and then with great feeling in a huge sweeping phrase, 'They seem to turn the faded leaves in this wood green again.'

Ex. 5

Bar 31 is the climax of the song, but it is a short-lived climax, for the vision fades and the tone with it; the accompaniment stepping down in 34, 35 (see Example 6) brings the singer back to earth. 'Des jours d'autrefois', as the composer indicates with his stresses, is a disillusionment not lightly or hastily passed over, but dwelt on with tender regret: one leaves the word 'jours' as if reluctant to go to the inevitable 'd'autrefois'. Debussy anticipated this by reminding us to adopt the first *tempo* again in 36.

Ex. 6

My pedalling creates the blurred effect of a mingled chime. It will be found that bars 37 and 39 if played softly will not jar unpleasingly; the bells die away in the distance, 'Past recall, past recall' they seem to say.

Reprinted by permission of Messrs. A. Durand & Son, Paris

L 3.00.008 Claire Croiza (Mme Meedintiano)
U BP1434 Pierre Bernac (J. Doyen)

MANDOLINE

Poem by PAUL VERLAINE   *Music by* CLAUDE DEBUSSY

SIR CHARLES HOLMES writes: 'Refining upon the somewhat gross revels of Rubens and other predecessors, Antoine Watteau paints human life as a courtly picnic: yet for all its splendour of silks and satins, for all its moods and its fervour, the company is fragile, insubstantial, pathetic.'

Much of Verlaine's poetry could be similarly described. Such verses as 'Clair de lune', 'Fantoches', and 'Mandoline' are in the Watteau style and attracted the attention of Debussy, Fauré, Reynaldo Hahn, and many others. The gay delightful Debussy song 'Mandoline' is simply an *al fresco* scene of gallants serenading fair ladies, exchanging 'des propos fades' under a rose and grey moon, whirling, dancing together to the tinkling accompaniment of the mandoline. The piano part is the mandoline except where Debussy uses it to describe the elegance of the ladies with their long trailing silken dresses

The first note is *pizzicato.* It is as if the player plucked the string of his instrument to warn the singers and dancers to make ready. I play the grace-note in the bass softly, but bang my finger with force on the treble G, and after the finger leaves the note I press down the sustaining pedal. Were I to use the pedal before my finger left the key the effect would be of a sustained note going through all the gradations of *ff, f, mf, mp,* to a *piano.* But Debussy's mark is *sf.p* and this cannot be done without a margin of time (the length of which depends on the pianoforte) between the release of the note by the finger and the depression of the pedal. I must admit that the strident *sforzando* is by no means reminiscent of a mandoline but I always hope the audience will forget this when their ears catch the soft rather distant overtone caught by the pedal. When I know my pianoforte I let this effect sink well into the audience's consciousness by observing the *fermata,* but I have known less fortunate occasions when I have failed to catch the tone with my pedal, in which case I conveniently forget the *fermata* and proceed hurriedly to the next bar.

Another way that this *sforzando-piano* can be obtained is to depress first the treble G without sounding the note, then, still holding it down, strike the lower G sharply and quickly with the left hand: the whole operation to be performed without the pedal.

49

The soft pedal can be held through the whole song—that is, from bar 2 onwards, provided it does not deaden the treble tinkle from bars 8 to 14; but apart from the effect we seek in the first bar and last bar, the sustaining pedal is wanted not at all, with two important exceptions.

The right-hand chords in Example 2 should be flicked, for all the world as if we were strumming a guitar or mandoline. I recommend a touch of the sustaining pedal in bars 11, 12, the soft left-hand chords can thus be joined, matching the singer's sighing on 'chanteuses' as seen in Example 3.

Actually a good performance of this song does depend very largely on the skill of the pianist, but the subtleties in the vocal part are as manifold, if less obvious. Debussy marked his scores so carefully that we can never be in any doubt as to his intentions. Take the vocal line in bars 4 and 5 (Ex. 1) and contrast the phrase with bars 6, 7, 'Les belles écouteuses' have a *legato* line and a graceful *crescendo diminuendo* denied to 'Les donneurs de sérénades'. The nuance does not call for warmth of feeling, it is just a bow to the ladies—ladies whose beauty while undeniable is less appreciated by the fact that the gallant is more concerned that his bow should be a graceful one. Again Debussy's care for detail should be noted from bars 8 to 13.

Ex. 3

The accent on 'fades' tells us how platitudinous were the compliments exchanged. The serenaders are Tircis and Aminte, both dismissed in three bars, and Clitandre (I cannot help feeling he was rather a bore) who has four bars all to himself.

Ex. 4

While Damis 'qui pour mainte Cruelle'

Ex. 5

arouses, to some extent, our sympathy. One feels he was an honest trier. In the latter phrase, no stress should be made on the top G in bar 24, the three notes on 'fait' should be shaped

Ex. A

rather than

Ex. B

but on 'tendre' a suggestion of a *rallentando* is quite desirable.

It will be seen from these quotations that the singer must pay great attention to detail. If the song be taken at too quick a *tempo* these inflexions will be lost; yet the song should not lose its liveliness: the detail is not more important than the whole. In any case this song does not go 'like the wind'; some people take it ridiculously fast whereas Debussy's instruction is *allegretto vivace*—not *presto* or even *allegro*. From bar 2 (for the pianist stays on bar 1 as long as he can) to bar 25 takes about thirty seconds.

The description of the ladies' elegance and their trailing draperies is drawn with long graceful sweeps in the accompaniment. Here the pianist discards the mandoline for the moment—he uses the sustaining pedal and with lightest touch brushes the notes in the treble.

Ex. 6

The pattern of the opening section returns and once again we are whirled away in chase of those shadowy figures whose tinkling mandoline and silvery laughter mingle with the breezes and are lost in the night. With quickening *tempo*, and tone becoming more and more inaudible, the song ends.

Reprinted by permission of Messrs. Durand & Son, Paris

O	123670	Roger Bourdin
U	BP1434	Pierre Bernac
C	74027	Lilian Nordica
G	DB709	Nellie Melba
V	1905	Lily Pons
Pat	PDT82	Ninon Vallin
D	K2333	Gérard Souzay
G	DA6013	M. Dubuis (S. Gyr)

THE NIGHTINGALE HAS A LYRE OF GOLD

Words by **W. E. HENLEY**   *Music by* **FREDERICK DELIUS**

THERE is no basic *tempo* for this song. The movement is influenced by the words, by the shape of the phrase, by the pianoforte writing under the voice. 'With easy movement' Delius says, and I think he uses the word 'easy' as the antithesis of 'tight'. *Rubato* is the order of the day. The first vocal phrase, for instance, 8–9–10 moves up impetuously to its highest note, but the next phrase 12–13–14 is not shaped in the same way. If the singer is over-impetuous here his partner will have his fingers tied in knots in a frantic attempt to articulate the lark's call (see Example 3). Not only that: if the singer uses too loud a tone here—Delius marks it *mezzoforte*—the accompanist's contribution will, in his effort to be heard, sound like an elephant crashing his way through the jungle. Whatever concession is thus made to the accompanist, is not on the grounds of technical difficulties that he may encounter—such considerations are unworthy—but purely that the listener can hear clearly what the song is about. The singer herself must be conscious of the birds' songs that are going on in the pianoforte, for they are the source of her inspiration.

Here is the *rubato* introduction; as irresponsible as a bird's flight.

You fly in the last three quavers of 1 on to the branch in 2 where you rest quietly and contentedly until you fly again in 3—to rest again in 4.

53

I have indicated where the movement is speeded up and where held
back; the expression marks are mine also. It does not matter how
leisurely your pace in the places where I have written 'wait', so long
as you urge forward with the arrows. The semiquaver chirrups at the
end of bars 4 and 6 must be brisk.

It is obvious that the same sustaining pedal cannot be used throughout the whole seven bars. The composer's instruction is delightfully
vague, it merely reads 'with pedal'. Evidently the pianist is intended
to use his own discretion. I have marked the pedalling which I
use.

A joyous singing tone is needed especially in bars 1 to 4. It would
be a pity to spread the bass chord in bar 1, and if the hand is too small
to contain it the simplest expedient is to take the top note with the
right hand. This can be done with the wide chord at 6 and at any
similar points. How frequently we send a boy on a man's errand by
attempting the impossible, by striving to play these large chords
with the left hand merely because they are written in the bass
clef! Let the right hand do a little extra work instead of lolling
idly by.

As I said, the singer sweeps up to the top note on 'gold' and in one
breath.

But she may have to breathe as marked (12 to 16) in the middle of
each of the next two phrases, as they are slower and more sustained.
All the same it is better not to break these phrases if the singer can
possibly manage them.

It can be seen by the foregoing example that 12 to 14 needs different treatment from 8 to 10. 'Call' is given plenty of space but we do not sweep up to it with the same precipitancy as we did up to 'gold'; it is a slower climb and the vocal line a steady one. There is a *diminuendo* from 16 to 18 (though the blackbird's *pianissimo* fluting in the accompaniment must be heard).

And now the singer goes mad, intoxicated by the joy of life and the mad spring weather, with no thought for the pianist. This is as it should be, for the latter must fly abreast of his partner playing his surging triplet chords with zest and verve, but remembering too that the singer —intoxicated or sober—will have to pause for a breath.

Ex. 4

This breath is taken after 'life' (23) and the danger is that in trying to maintain the quick *tempo* the singer will take in a hurried gulp of air, skimping the quaver B sharp and rendering the word 'life' so unintelligibly that the wondering listener hears only—what sounds to him like—

the 'joy of lie'. Decidedly it is better to stress this quaver slightly, allowing the consonant at the end of the word to be heard, taking time for
the breath and then soaring ahead again. The pianist must be aware
of the singer's intentions in this matter; his heart of course is full of 'joie
de vivre' but his brain is not befuddled by it.

Delius was a little unkind to place the word 'spring' on those high
notes in 25, and some singers have the greatest difficulty in making the
word clear. Like 'joy', in the previous phrase, it is the most important
word in this phrase, and the crowning point of the quick section. If the
singer sacrifices word value for tone value the listener is apt to hear
'and we in the mad spray weather'—which has a damping effect. I have
heard singers evade the issue in this manner:

Ex. 4a

Apart from the fact that the composer did not write it thus, there is the
more practical objection that the quick quaver again gives the word
'spring' a poor chance. However, it is an idea, and if singers put it to
practical use I advise them to make a wholehearted *tenuto* on this quaver
and to invest the consonants with great energy, using the S-P-R as a
sort of springboard before diving into the vowel. The accompanist
'treads water' during the singer's preliminaries on the springboard,
prepared to wait as long as is necessary for the clear enunciation of
the word.

Delius brings the song to a most beautiful close. From 27 onwards
the music sinks to a calmer, quieter ecstasy. After the breathless joy of
22 to 26 the singer will not find it easy to keep the tone steady during
this long-drawn-out sweetness. In fact she is immediately confronted by
a phrase so long and sustained that it will be wellnigh impossible to
accomplish in one breath; I give it with the composer's expression
marks, though the breaths in 28 and 31 are mine.

Ex. 5

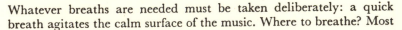

Whatever breaths are needed must be taken deliberately: a quick
breath agitates the calm surface of the music. Where to breathe? Most

certainly not after 'sang' (29); a breath here spoils the lovely line of the voice, C sharp, A, B flat (I like the suspicion of an *apportamento* on the major third interval in 29), and in addition it betrays a misunderstanding of the poet's meaning, for the verb 'sang' is used to infer 'joined' or 'fused'. And this is why I would take my breath after 'listened', enabling me to come out with a full heart on the *mezzoforte* 'till he sang our hearts and lips'—a deliberate breath, then *mezzopiano*—'together'. If you do not need a breath in 31 so much the better, but 'together' must be firm—and this injunction includes the last syllable.

Bars 37 to 40 give the pianist the rounding off of the song. It is an enviable chance for these bars are full of colour, full of love. Yes, you love them as you play them.

There is a big step down in tone from the *piano* of 37, 38 to the *pp* of 39, 40. So quiet are the last two bars that the accompanying chords under the melody are felt rather than heard. After the 'slower' of 27 and the 'still slower' of 28, the composer again says 'slower' in 37 so that we know we can take all the time in the world over this postlude. I make a *fermata* on the third beat of 38 letting the tone die before the *pp* in 39. We linger long over these bars, sorry that the song has to end. They are real Delius and no other composer could have written them.

C L2344   Dora Labbette (Sir Thomas Beecham)

EL PAÑO MORUNO

Music by MANUEL DE FALLA

'THE Moorish Cloth' is one of a group of seven Spanish songs set by
de Falla; it reads 'Should this precious fabric by some evil chance become stained, its value would be completely lost.' The warning applies
to something deeper, something less tangible than a piece of tapestry
and is, I believe, an allegorical allusion to the purity of a maiden.
Should she lose her virtue, should her chastity be violated: but no! I will
pursue the damsel no further. The standard of morals amongst the
Moors is extremely high, and I eagerly pay tribute to it: beyond this,
however, I am bound to say that I can see no connexion whatever
between the words and the vivacious dance rhythm of the piano part.
On the other hand the voice has a melancholy strain and a *legato* line
which implies that the singer seems to fear the worst. It holds itself
aloof, withdrawn into its own shell, uninfluenced by the spirited *staccato*
of the accompaniment. This melancholy is thrown up in relief by reason
of its total disregard of the piano part; and this contrast between the
moods of voice and piano gives the song its impact. But the music
must be allowed to speak for itself without the singer 'doing anything
to it'.

Despite the *pianissimo* sign at the beginning, the introduction scintillates from first note to last.

58

It is possible, while still maintaining an *allegretto vivace*, to play all this sluggishly. There are three ways such a pass can be avoided.

We know that the lilt of a Viennese waltz is not obtained by a flat-footed adherence to a solid three beats to the bar, there is a suggestion of a hiatus between the second and third beats, a slight rhythmic lift which renders it distinctive from any other style of waltz music. No connexion whatever exists between the character of this Spanish dance we are studying and the Viennese, except that *rubato* is used in both cases but is applied in a different way. If I were to exaggerate, the effect would be something like this:

Ex. 1a

But this, I emphasize, is a great exaggeration of the rhythmic shape, for it is impossible to write down in our notation what should be the slightest of suggestions. This elasticity or stretching gives muscle to the music. It is inert without it. The pianist, therefore, in the first place makes his semiquavers virile like the rat-tat of a pair of heels on the floor—but he never loses sight of the third beat. Secondly he observes that bars 1 to 15 have a bass that is *pizzicato*, except for 4, 8, 12 which are *arco*. Finally, of course, the verve and sparkle that this athletic rhythm demands depend on the temperament and dash which the pianist puts into it. The *crescendo*, 20 to 23, is a vigorous one (I play the top note of the final chord with the left hand) but prior to this it is all submerged excitement save for *poco crescendi* at 5 and 13.

The singer should warn her partner to get his violent chord well out of the way before she makes her entry—therefore, no pedal is wanted on this chord so that the voice will be heard singing *cantabile* without any break in the tempo.

Playing this song for Victoria de los Angeles recently, I was struck by the cool detachment with which she sang it. The effect of her calm leisurely *legato* line floating serenely above the *pizzicato*, unaffected by the energetic introduction, was quite extraordinary. Surely therefore if this Spanish artist, full of temperament though she is, controls her excitement and performs the song in a cool and unruffled manner, that is the very manner in which to perform it. I believe many singers' initial error is putting too much gusto into it; they are influenced by the accompaniment especially if the latter is well played. Looking at the voice part

Ex. 2

it can readily be appreciated how easy it is to magnify de Falla's stresses, to over-emphasize his non-adhesive quavers (25, 29) to surge violently up a rising phrase and vice versa, to imbue the whole affair with an excess of emotion. Yet one can be misled by the *grazioso e leggiero*. These instructions must be obeyed but the vocal line must be firm and have an over-all *legato*. Extreme care is needed at 26, 30 and more especially at 34, 37 to see that no intrusive H makes its ubiquitous appearance.

At 46 the accompanist flicks his chord like the crack of a whip, but once again it is without sustaining pedal, to enable the singer to maintain her calm *piano* tone.

Ex. 3

A sigh terminates the song, and here, at last, the singer is allowed to evince some emotion.

Ex. 4

A Spanish piece of music is often made the vehicle for a display of temperamental extravagance on the part of the performer: because it is Spanish he or she assumes it must be fiery and untidy; angry splashes of colour, careless distortions of essential rhythm are invoked to give a cloak of authenticity. But this is all very wide of the mark. That great man Pau Casals never performs Spanish music with reckless abandon, his interpretations are refined, well-ordered, poetic; there is no room in his world for the coarse or vulgar.

'El Paño Moruno' is refined. The suggestion behind the words is veiled and extremely delicate, and the singer will win praise who studies it as conscientiously as she studies Mozart or Scarlatti, and sings it with the same care.

Though this set of songs requires a voice of 'Mediterranean timbre' (Victoria de los Angeles for example), a singer has not necessarily to be Spanish in order to do it justice, and the name of Joan Hammond leaps to my mind instantly as the type of brilliant and thrilling voice that is needed.

Reprinted by permission of Max Eschig, Paris, and of J. & W. Chester Ltd.

C   D11701   Maria Barrientos (Manuel de Falla)
P   P0153   Conchita Supervia (Frank Marshall)

C	4575X	Conchita Velasquez
G	DB9731	Victoria de los Angeles (Gerald Moore)
D	AX197	Nancy Evans (Hubert Foss)
V	12-0334	C. Torres (J. Newmark)
G	DA1928	Victoria de los Angeles (Gerald Moore)
Pat	X3460	Ninon Vallin
G	EG6097	S. del Campo
G	DA5038	S. Tavares (R. Machado)
D	LX3077	Gérard Souzay (Jacqueline Bonneau)

L'INVITATION AU VOYAGE

Words by CH. BAUDELAIRE   *Music by* HENRI DUPARC

IN this poem we float along in a dream world of magic contentment; the very waves bearing us to the haven of beauty and of peace are unreal. We gaze again and again and cannot describe what we see but know that it is moving, beautiful, strange, insubstantial. It is ecstasy.

As Baudelaire casts a spell like a pipe-dream one is hardly aware of the words—mere words—with which he does it, so Duparc weaves a web of notes—mere notes—into a dazzling pattern of sound.

Duparc's setting of this poem is glorious, but it is one thing to be inspired with an idea and quite another to have to put it down in black and white. Pity the poor composer! How open to misconception his inspiration can be when the performer is unable to probe below the surface of the printed page.

An interesting parallel to this song's introduction can be seen in Schubert's 'Nacht und Träume'.

This accompaniment, when truly appreciated by the player, is most beautiful, but a cursory glance—by way of becoming acquainted with it—is certainly not enough to lay bare the composer's idea, in fact it can very easily be played in such a way that it becomes heavy, coarse, and lumpy. I recommend the student in the course of his practising to play the above example in a careless, heavy-handed, unimaginative way and without the sustaining pedal. The effect of this will (it is to be hoped) make him shudder with horror. Let him then get below the surface of the notes, let him soak himself in the poem, let him achieve the *legato* by use of the pedal, and the *pianissimo* that Schubert wanted, and let him listen critically to himself; above all let him listen with love and then perhaps he will experience a glow which tells him he is near to Schubert's heart.

Here then is Duparc's start to 'L'invitation au Voyage'. The blurred impressionistic effect that Schubert wanted is also wanted here, only psychologically do they differ, one being dark (note the low *tessitura* of the Schubert accompaniment) and the other light. But the technical means to achieve the two are the same.

Ex.1

The sustaining pedal is held throughout each bar—how else can Duparc's pedal point in the bass which persists for nearly fifty bars sing through? In bars 2, 4, 6, 8, &c. this soft bass diapason is lost because of the change of pedal but the continual reiteration of the bass in the odd-numbered bars really deceives the ear into believing it is really there all the time. (On a modern pianoforte with three pedals, the centre pedal sustains these bass notes and this pedal is of vital help here since it will carry the pedal point through the even-numbered bars, singing independently without clashing with the treble.)

There are twelve semiquavers to each bar and most certainly twelve semiquavers must be played. Yet the player will let us *feel* these rather than let us be aware of each individual note. The fingers are touching the keys all the time, but never is the key struck, the tone is coaxed from the instrument and thus a smooth shimmer is effected. But an amateur pianist, reading what I have said, who thinks I am recommending the omission of an odd note here and there merely because I do not want the accompaniment to sound like a ticking clock, is very much mistaken.

It is essential that no angles or points appear in the accompaniment; any percussiveness or departure from the smooth ripple will be most disturbing to the singer. And yet the latter with his soaring vocal line needs substantial support from the piano. When I remind the reader that I described this song as insubstantial it seems that I now contradict myself: let us look once again at 'Nacht und Träume'.

Ex. B

On 'Lust', a long held note, the music asks for a *crescendo* and the accompanist swells with the singer. This is done quite easily and without percussiveness if the sustaining pedal is held firmly down and more and more pressure is given to each succeeding semiquaver. Above all I impress on the player the necessity to see to it that his fingers are always *touching the keys*. Each note is allowed to rise from its key-bed after it has spoken for as soon as we hear it sing the pressure on it immediately becomes so slight that the finger is almost pushed up by the key. When the player hears his tone swelling he can, still keeping his sustaining pedal down, make his *diminuendo*; he can do this even before the *diminuendo* is marked since the overtones which the sustaining pedal sets free are still reverberating. This wonderful swelling effect is so gentle and insidious that the listener is hardly aware it has occurred until he hears that the pianoforte tone is dying down again. Time and time again in 'L'invitation au Voyage' the pianist employs this same method in support of his partner. Its effect will give the singer the feeling that there is substantial support underneath him; yet the listener will be aware of nothing substantial beyond the long low boom of the bass.

The singer feels he is floating on the smoothest stream with nothing to jar, nothing to unsettle him. He is completely relaxed (or appears to be) and we are able to listen to him at our ease, unconscious of the difficulties and occasional strenuousness of his part. So free and soaring is the vocal line that one is surprised to find it is practically all within the compass of one octave.

For English-speaking singers the French language seems to present insuperable difficulties and yet the literature of French songs is so rich and so varied that the singer of courage and determination must tackle it. Surely the gramophone record played again and again—if the singer be a Bernac, a Panzéra, a Souzay, a Danco—cannot fail to give the keen-eared student a key to the authentic inflexion and accent. (In their excursions abroad, our singers limit themselves far too readily to a return ticket to Vienna, but Paris and Rome are enchanting too. Take Mark Raphael; he yields to none in his love of Wolf but he sings Fauré and Alessandro Scarlatti with equal devotion and facility.)

It can be seen in Example 1 that if the singer is going to begin softly and tenderly, his part will be submerged when its *tessitura* lies below the level of the pianoforte unless the accompaniment is a real *pianissimo*. The singer must see to this, since accompanists are apt to forget that their treble here is in a strong register of the keyboard. He must also demand an increase of tone from the accompanist (it should really be instinctive but is not marked) at 8 and 9.

Pierre Bernac, who sings this song so beautifully, does not breathe in bar 4. He observes the quaver rest of course, but breathes after 'sœur' and after 'douceur' where Duparc has put a comma.

One section of the song, unutterably calm and lovely, I give in its entirety.

Ex. 2 *Un peu plus vite*

Most singers make the mistake of slowing up the *tempo* here, as, for the first time, the waves are still and we seem to float in mid-air: but thanks to Duparc's clear instruction 'un peu plus vite' there is no sense of stagnation; we are wafted along. The tone here must be clear and without any unsteadiness, and yet in spite of the feeling of ecstatic bliss, the singer delivers these bars with an underlying intensity to impress them on the listener's memory so that they will be recognized when they recur in a slightly varied form at the end of the song. This refrain is significant above all else; its *pianissimo*, the singer's monotone, its high almost inaudible treble in the accompaniment so far above its bass *point d'orgue*, all contribute to a marvellous reflexion of the poem's atmosphere. And the accompanist rests for a long time, a very long time, on his *fermata* before allowing the stillness of the major chord to merge into the minor, where the current takes hold again and bears us along as of old.

In Example 3 we see a contrapuntal tune in the pianoforte; it is played with a resolute tone to support the singer, and the accompanist listens intently to 'Ton moindre' so that the A flat and the G can be expanded with some freedom by his partner.

Ex. 3

Then, as if to make amends for having deserted his pedal point for four consecutive bars, the left hand plunges with a resounding splash on to the bass octave in 54. This sojourn in the depths is but short-lived, for at 58 the accompaniment in a series of glittering *arpeggi* seems to be reflecting the glancing lights of the setting sun. Up to 57 the playing has been as smooth as glass; it has been unobtrusive in spite of the occasional excursions into a *forte*, but now at 58 the effect is altogether more dazzling and brilliant. In growing exaltation the singer responds to this urge and he makes sure that his tone carries high and clear over these cascades.

After a glorious climax, like a giant wave (Dans une chaude lumière), the music quietens, and once more we hear the refrain of Example 2 but this time to a softly rippling accompaniment. Now we see how important it was to deliver Example 2 with sensibility; the listener recognizes the intention behind it, sees its inevitability and logic.

The accompaniment with ever gentler motion guides us to this haven of loveliness we are seeking until, with the faintly heard chord at the very end, we know that we have reached our harbour.

Ex. 4

En diminuant jusqu'à la fin

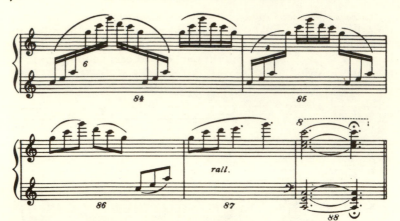

Reprinted by permission of Editions Rouart-Lerolle & Co., Paris

G	DB4819	Charles Panzéra (Mme Panzéra-Baillot)
C	D15041	Claire Croiza (Francis Poulenc)
C	D12027	Marthe Nespoulous
G	JG178	Maggie Teyte
G	DB6312	Pierre Bernac (Francis Poulenc)
C	72050D	Lily Pons
C	ML4258	Martial Singher (Paul Ulanowsky)
G	DB10035	P. Sandoz (P. Baumgartner)
Pat	X7230	Ninon Vallin
O	123553	David Davries
V	12-1251	Dorothy Maynor

CLAIR DE LUNE

(Menuet)

Poem by PAUL VERLAINE   *Music by* GABRIEL FAURÉ
Op. 46 No. 2

DISCUSSING George Butterworth's 'Loveliest of Trees' I suggested that it was the type of song which can bear the imprint of the singer's personality upon it. His imagination, his sense of colour, shape, and poetry can be brought into play. Butterworth gives the performer a comparatively free rein, always of course with the assumption that his trust will not be abused, that this freedom will be kept within bounds by taste and musicianship. (Without these qualities no singer is worth listening to.) I suggested, also, that some music should be left to speak for itself and was impaired by the intrusion of the singer's personality. To this category Fauré's 'Clair de Lune' belongs.

Mesmerized by this song's enchantment, the most virtuous singer is tempted to infuse too much warmth into the tone; tempted to colour with nuances the music's gentle rises and soft falls; induced to underline a word or stress a note. Most of the song wants a *voix blanche*, and should be performed with all the *legato* that singer and pianist can give. We do not want to feel when listening to 'Clair de Lune' that it is being 'interpreted' for us. There is no room for any personal idiosyncrasy, therefore the *tempo* is always strict, ruling out any idea of *rubato*. In short, we sing here almost without expression, for thus only, paradoxically, does the song become truly expressive of the poet's and composer's meaning.

Fauré, like most great song writers, makes his accompaniments of equal importance with the voice, indeed in 'Clair de Lune' the piano often carries the tune while the singer supplies an *obligato*. The charming piano part does not present insuperable problems to the accompanist for it lies gratefully under the fingers, yet it needs sensitive playing. Mood and *tempo* are established in the introduction. I think, as I play it, of the moon under whose cold light the masked dancers are gliding; remembering 'Ils n'ont pas l'air de croire à leur bonheur' and that 'Tout enchantant sur le mode mineur'—'quasi tristes'. Excepting bars 7 and 8 where there is a minute rise and fall, the tone should remain level all through this introduction.

In spite of the *legato*, the pianist takes the greatest care that his sustaining pedal creates no blur, and that in the treble the articulation is clear. The left hand accompanies the tune discreetly, gliding in after

71

Ex. 1 *Andantino quasi allegretto*

the beat without accent. Once again it must be insisted that the introduction, including the nuance in 7–8, is played in strict time.

I hope the singer will not feel I am doing him an injustice by saying
that he supplies an *obligato*. I perhaps redeem myself in his eyes by
stating unequivocally that his task is far harder than his partner's. He
has to keep his tone pure and unemotional, a tone thin rather than
substantial which maintains an even flow through the long phrases; his
words, demanding an almost precious enunciation, must not conflict
with his *legato* line; on the other hand this desire for smoothness should
not jeopardize his crystal-clear enunciation. His obedience to the text
will ensure that the little *crescendi* and *diminuendi*—most sparingly used
by Fauré—are not exaggerated. Indeed there is a faint air of *insouciance*
about the vocal part.

All this has to be accomplished with complete ease and relaxation;
at least that is the impression the singer should give us.

Ex. 2   *dolce*

Tout   en chan-tant, sur le mo-de mi-neur,
      26   27

When the singer sings the above example we feel that he floats up there without effort. It would be very easy to make a *crescendo* up to this top note, but the phrase is marked *dolce* and *pianissimo*, and therein lies its difficulty. The singer takes it in his stride giving us no evidence of any marshalling of forces that so often accompanies the attack on a high note or the beginning of a climax: the set facial expression, the tenseness of tone.

One feels that Fauré intentionally introduces the voice rather parenthetically at 12. Certainly the singer glides in without impact, so gently that he might have been singing several bars earlier without our noticing it.

Ex. 3

At all events he does not give the listener any indication in 11 or 12 that his entry is impending by moving his lips as he breathes or heaving his chest (as much as to say 'Behold! I am about to sing').

Only at 16 does the composer depart from his precise quavers and semiquavers by a triplet in the third beat.

Ex. 4

This is the only triplet in the song. I draw attention to it because some singers make the mistake of singing 'mode mineur' (Ex. 2, bar 27) as if it too were a triplet.

Strangely enough one often hears a beautifully executed triplet on 'mode mineur' where it is not wanted, but the bar 16 triplet presents an unaccountable difficulty.

No slowing down of the tempo is wanted as the singer finishes, neither should the accompanist make a conventional *rallentando* as he ends the postlude. This 'matter-of-factness', incongruous though it may appear, adds to the fantastic quality of the music.

The lines of 'Clair de Lune' are neither bold nor colourful, but they are so cold, clear-cut, precise, that they leave no room for the faintest possibility of insipidity. This is a song of pale and tranquil beauty.

Reprinted by permission of Messrs. J. Hamelle & Co., Paris

G	DA4874	Eidé Noréna
P	R020094	Ninon Vallin (P. Darck)
G	DA4887	Charles Panzéra (Mme Panzéra-Baillot)
C	D12028	Marthe Nespoulous
G	DA1876	Maggie Teyte (Gerald Moore)
C	LF154	Georges Thill (Maurice Faure)
Pat	X93120	Alice Raveau
D	M606	Gérard Souzay (Jacqueline Bonneau)
G	E452	Anne Thursfield (Ivor Newton)
Sel	LPG8006	P. Mollet (P. Verger)
Van	VRS414	H. Cuenod (J. Blancard)

LYDIA

Poem by LECONTE DE LISLE   *Music by* GABRIEL FAURÉ

GABRIEL FAURÉ's purity of style and aristocratic manner sometimes cloak but never hide the urgency of feeling that lies under the refined surface of his music. If Debussy painted, Fauré sculpted. He was a master of shape; of curve and proportion. His clear line, polished and unyielding, may seem as cold as marble to the seeker for splashes of colour and unrestrained sentiment, but vehement expression or rhetorical grandiloquence were shunned by Fauré. He moves us, much more subtly, by reticent suggestion. In my opinion the beautiful poetry of Verlaine, Baudelaire, Leconte de Lisle, find their highest expression, generally speaking, in the songs of Gabriel Fauré. He is immersed in the poem, but he never allows his lyricism and suavity to be enslaved by it. I cannot think of another composer whose style is at once so simple and so individual. One could occasionally, perhaps excusably, mistake Ravel for Debussy, Schumann for Schubert, Beethoven for Haydn, but you cannot mistake Fauré. Nobody but he could have written the phrase with which 'Lydia' begins.

If you do not like these six bars then you do not like Fauré: the very essence of him is here.

Throughout the song, which is a two-verse strophic, the soprano part in the accompaniment moves in unison with the voice. While Fauré makes use of this expedient sometimes in his songs, it would be equally true to say that there are many more occasions when the accompaniment and the voice, though belonging warmly to one another, move with an independence that would have delighted the heart of Hugo Wolf. I stress the unison which occurs here only to emphasize the necessity for the two performers to wander along in sensitive intimacy, hand in hand.

Maggie Teyte loved singing this song, both for the sake of the music itself and for the technician's pleasure in negotiating the problems it poses. The delicate vocal line needs the firmest support from the singer. Breath should be firm but the voice should be, as the composer says, *dolce*. Only the rise and fall of the phrase, acknowledged by a slight *crescendo* and *diminuendo*, as shown in bars 4, 5, 6 and elsewhere, mark any change from the general *piano* which prevails throughout. The enunciation should be incisive, consonants distinct, without marring the *legato*; so that 'sur tes roses joues, et sur ton col frais et si blanc' can shoot forward on to the lips. Despite the 'Oue je puisse mourir' the tone should be bright: a darkening of a vowel will give the impression of flatness, and it is very easy to sag below the note in this song.

Ex. 2

Le jour qui luit est le meil-leur, Ou-bli-ons l'é-ter-nel-le tom - be,
11   *12*   *13*   *14*

A singer can see perhaps by the above a sample of the difficulties that abound and will also appreciate how a forward bright tone will make his task easier.

At the beginning of this attempt to describe 'Lydia' I used the word —unyielding. Rhythmically we must be unyielding where Fauré is concerned, for he disliked and distrusted *rubato*, therefore the singer should resist the temptation to treat bars 5 and 6 or bars 11 and 12 in a *rubato* manner. The slightest prolongation of a note at the top of a curve is often desirable if it is done tastefully, but this sort of treatment should nearly always be avoided in this composer's works. Indeed half the charm in the music is to be found in the strict observance of the instructions. In 'Lydia' there are two *rallentandi* at 18 and 35 and apart from these, the song always moves forward smoothly.

As usual in music of this tender intimacy, the piano moving with the voice, it is necessary for the pianist to judge to a nicety his tone to match the singer's. He need not be afraid to make the soprano voice in the accompaniment heard so long as he is not percussive, for he has the hope—always nourished by a good accompanist—that the listener, hearing the piano tone merging with the voice, will hardly be able to distinguish the one from the other. Perhaps the task he sets himself is an impossible one but he always aims for it. Of course the listener will be quickly undeceived if he occasionally hears the piano lagging behind the voice, or vice versa. The two performers glide forward as one, and this is the accompanist's responsibility. In any song of this nature he is, metaphorically, on his toes, alive, listening keenly, anticipating what the singer is going to do.

Lazy listening or a momentary carelessness on the pianist's part can disfigure this graceful phrase.

De Lisle's flowered words are saved from any semblance of artificiality by Fauré's simple treatment. 'Lydia' is an utterly charming song. It will move us, so long as the singer really obeys Fauré's instructions and does not try to stamp it with his own ego.

I ought to call attention to Fauré's charming pun, for 'Lydia' is written in the Lydian mode; that is, the sharpened fourth. Without the C sharp it would be unbearably drab.

Reprinted by permission of Messrs. J. Hamelle & Co., Paris

G	DA4878	Charles Panzéra (Mme Panzéra-Baillot)
O	188634	Roger Bourdin
PD	561022	Charles Rousseliere
G	DA1831	Maggie Teyte (Gerald Moore)
G	DA4931	Pierre Bernac (Francis Poulenc)

COME AWAY, COME AWAY, DEATH

('*Twelfth Night*')

Words by WILLIAM SHAKESPEARE   *Music by* GERALD FINZI

THIS composer's Shakespeare settings carry such an air of authenticity
in every bar that the listener is convinced they would have been accept-
able to an Elizabethan audience. Contradictorally enough Finzi is
essentially a twentieth-century product yet his music has the line and
the logic pleasing to the Victorian, it has the wit and freedom pleasing
to the all-wise young intellectual. The one can hear this music without
raising his eyebrows, the other without looking down his nose.

'Come away, Death' has a processional grandeur reminiscent of
Arne though it is simpler in conception. Indeed I should say at a rough
guess (for I do not know Gerald Finzi personally) that he is a keen
student of the old master: they have a passion, pathos, and humour
very much in common. This is not to question the legitimacy of our
contemporary's offspring, for there is originality in his every bar: but
I think he would nominate Arne as godfather. Finzi is in the great line
of English song writers.

Look at the first few bars and you will see the quality of man with
whom we are dealing.

That's good enough for anybody! It is a great phrase to sing with its impetuous semiquavers and its lordly drop on to 'death', all done in one breath above the march of the great bass chords booming like a funeral knell. Yes, one breath gives nobility to the sweeping phrase, though the less ambitious singer may have to refresh himself after bar 5—but on no account after bar 6, for the voice must drop from the A to the B. The same ukase applies in many instances through the song, for instance at bars 13, 14, 15 the singer does not give verisimilitude to the words by expelling his breath lustily; on the contrary.

Ex. 2

Again at 31 there is a comma after 'death', it is excusable to take a breath here, but how preferable to accomplish it without doing so, as the composer clearly wishes.

Ex. 3

As an example of the demands made on the singer's breathing technique I give the final phrase of the song: 'Lay me, O where sad true lover never find my grave'—and then:

Ex. 4

This beautiful phrase, all *pianissimo*, finishing as firmly as it began, would be spoiled by an aching void the while air was being hastily gulped. I do not wish to cast a damper on the enthusiastic amateur who will derive great enjoyment from singing this song. Let him breathe when he will rather than shun it, but in Example 4 it is preferable that he should hasten the movement rather than interrupt its flow. Naturally we do not expect the professional to give in so easily.

Just as it is taken for granted that the accompanist has his eye on the vocal line, his ear on his partner, so is it equally essential for the singer to be intimately aware of what is going on in the piano part, even while he is giving voice. It should be part and parcel of himself. Ernest Newman once said—I quote from memory—that one could sometimes tell by the colour of Gerhardt's tone whether the harmony underlying her note was major or minor. A fine artist, no matter if he cannot play the piano himself, studies the piano part and all it signifies. This statement is so obvious and so elementary that I am almost ashamed to write it: and yet I know that some singers (and professionals at that) through laziness or lack of musicality, wallow in blissful ignorance, content to dwell in splendid isolation so far as their partner at the piano is concerned. There are many instances in this song where the accompaniment has clanging dissonances and sombre shades calculated to affect the sensitive singer's tone. He feels

Ex. 5

through his body the stab of the B flat on 'cypress' (9) and 'slain' (17). 'Stuck all with yew', 'no one so true', and Example 4 are similar instances where the iron of the accompanying harmonies enters the singer's soul, and entering, will do something to him. Yes, these harmonies set up a mental vibration which, literally, changes the quality of the voice. I cannot explain this in technical terms, it is too metaphysical for me to cope with. I only know that when a singer and accompanist work and think along these lines with devoted perseverance these things happen.

O MISTRESS MINE

('*Twelfth Night*')

Words by WILLIAM SHAKESPEARE   *Music by* GERALD FINZI

WHENEVER I play this song, I think of lads and lasses on some English village green, dancing to the sound of the fiddle. (Most improper of me, no doubt, I ought to picture the Sylvan glade of Illyria and a consort of viols, but the reader will have to be indulgent at my insularity and lack of perspective.) Here in Finzi's song I insist we have fiddlers, and amateurs at that: for the bowing arm is stiff and the style rustic. Though the playing is always light and amiable, and roughness avoided, no attempt should be made to round off the corners since the music is intentionally square. In only seven bars of the song is the sustaining pedal really wanted (29 to 31 and 55 to 58), for the remainder, the chords in the left hand are uniformly *pizzicato* thus throwing all the onus on the right hand, for here we are fairly consistently *legato*.

82

It can be seen how extremely difficult without the pedal's help the treble becomes. In its efforts to maintain a smooth line the hand clings to the keys like an organist's and crawls crab-like from one chord to the next. The two voices in the soprano clef are always clearly heard over the springy, zestful bass, the upper voice does not outshine the lower, they are each distinct, each determined to be heard. Any chance that the treble has of a *staccato* it seizes with avidity, at 2 for instance it skips up, prior to the stressed chord, like a dancer.

Robert Irwin, who first introduced me to the Finzi settings of Shakespeare and Thomas Hardy, sang this song with debonair charm. He was content, it seemed to me, to let his voice rise only a little above the tonal level of the accompaniment, the latter was in no danger of being submerged. This example should be followed by all singers of 'O Mistress Mine' otherwise the dance tune will have to be played more sharply to be heard, and the village fiddler only uses the middle of the bow.

Ex. 2

No *rallentando* precedes the voice's entry. The singer's *legato* flows serenely over the humorous *staccato* chords. He does not breathe after 'mine' otherwise his *crescendo*, made independently of the accompaniment, would lose its effect. As can be seen in the above and following examples the phrases, seeming at first glance to be short, are deceptively protracted, there is quite a long note waiting for the singer at the end of each, for which he must be ready.

Ex. 3

We get a picture of the maid who has captured our fancy by the Example 4 (page 84), with its delicious little syncopation at bar 24: she can be seen tripping o'er the lea.

Ex. 4

I like too, in the second verse, the accompaniment's subtle suggestion of doubt at the words 'What's to come is still unsure'.

Ex. 5

As I have said, the sustaining pedal comes into play at 55 to 58 and also at the conclusion of verse 1.

Ex. 6

Again the long note at the end of the vocal phrase, the while the accompaniment hops merrily onward (59). Without doubt 57 is quizzical, but despite the *pianissimo* it does not lose its eagerness; after all there is urgency in the words. The amount of urgency the performer puts into it depends largely on his own personal outlook: I, being no longer in the first flush of youth, regard this bar most seriously but I do not criticize a youngster for singing it with easy nonchalance—I only envy.

It can be seen in the examples here and also in 'Come away, Death' how generous is Finzi's vocal line. The voice part is not carefully nursed but frequently contains wide intervals and octave leaps, yet it is always grateful. These songs require, fundamentally, fine honest singing. They are healthy.

Sir Arnold Bax said, 'Try everything once: everything, that is, except folk-dancing.' But this song almost converts me, for though every bar of it be original, you can see boys and girls dancing round the Maypole to its strains. At all events it is deeply rooted in England, and none the worse for that.

Reprinted by permission of Messrs. Boosey & Hawkes Ltd.

EL MAJO DISCRETO

('Tonadilla')

Words by E. PERIQUET   Music by E. GRANADOS

EDWARD SACKVILLE-WEST and Desmond Shawe-Taylor in *The Record Guide* (Collins) describe a Tonadilla as 'a type of Spanish song popular in the eighteenth century, generally sung during theatrical interludes, and often satirical in tone'. Granados wrote a dozen or more Tonadillas but I have chosen this one because it is one of the favourites of the brilliant Victoria de los Angeles.

'It is possible that my love is ugly,' says the singer, 'but after all love is blind. Let others think what they like about his looks, to me he has a more precious quality; he is discretion itself and he knows how to keep a secret.'

Granados not only writes with disarming simplicity but he is very economical with his expression marks. The singer bears in mind that the writing is in the folk-music style. The refined and musicianly rises and falls of tone so desirable in a deeply felt Schubert phrase are not wanted here, where every note must have the sparkle of sunshine, the tone a hard brilliance rather than a soft radiance.

The soul of all Spanish music is in its rhythm. When as a young man I studied Albeniz, de Falla, Granados and other Spanish composers, I felt instinctively that there was something mysterious about their rhythm, some secret about their *rubato* that a stranger to Spain would find extremely difficult to solve. Intensive study and soaking in it is of course necessary to arrive at terms of intimacy, but there is no trick about it. Association with Casals, Suggia, Cassado and d'Alvarez taught me that the music must sound simple. I advise the student approaching these quick-moving and virile dances for the first time to play the notes exactly as the composer has written them and to observe the strictest time. When one has, after study and thought, arrived on terms of intimacy with this music, it is then that the slightest suggestion of *rubato*, as I said in my remarks on 'El paño moruno', can be employed. And this *rubato* is only occasional, illustrative it may be of the snap of a finger or the rat-tat of the heel.

When, therefore, you come to sing the following Examples 1 and 2, the quaver in 10 and the quaver rest in 12 are precise, the triplet in 15 is so clear it almost clicks like a castanet. The vocal part in the second verse is a slight variation of the first, and Example 2 shows what Granados does with it. Crystal clear quavers are wanted. There

Ex. 1

Di - en que mi ma - joes fe - o
10 11 12 13

Es po - si - ble que si que lo se - a
14 15 16 17

Ex. 2

Mas si no es mi ma - jo un hom - bre
31 32 33

que por lin - do des cue - lle y a som - bre
34 35 36 37

is no need for the singer to feel that a heavy *legato* is essential (it can be seen that the composer gives an occasional *legato* sign which must be observed) in the first verse, for she is all over the stave at 18 to 22.

Ex. 3

Que a-mor es de - se - o que cie - ga y ma - re - a
18 19 20 21 22

I do not want it thought for a moment that I advocate a *staccato* here, I only suggest that the line needs such a fresh and vital attack that an oleaginous smoothness is out of the question and out of character.

In the second verse, as can be seen in Example 2, and in the example below, which is a variation of Example 3, Granados gives the singer every opportunity by his 'quaver-joining' for a smoother line.

Ex. 4

En cam - bio es dis - cre - to y guar - da un se - cre - to
38 39 40 41 42

With the transition to the relative minor, the composer asks for a real *legato*, and here the line is much more accommodating for it, and the mood momentarily less flippant.

But the song finishes with its former sparkle, and a rousing top note that will gladden the heart of any singer or listener.

Ex. 5

Victoria de los Angeles makes a slight *fermata* on 74 but the *tempo* must be taken up smartly and pertly at 75–76 with the accompanist giving a good accent for finality's sake on his bass octave.

This is the type of accompaniment which repays a little thought, though it is very difficult to persuade most accompanist of the truth of such a statement, for they esteem it an utter waste of time to give any consideration to these bars.

Ex. 6

Be it understood that the pianist is imitating a guitar, yet on the other hand he must infuse the same sparkle and vitality into his part that the singer puts into hers; to do this let the sustaining pedal be ignored, let the bass note be given its exact value of one beat, give a slight accent on the second beat and make the quavers click like castanets.

There are two delightful interludes for the pianist and he tries to get colour and life into these by playing 46 to 50 with pedal and in a *mezzoforte* whereas Example 7, 51 to 54, are played *molto, staccato* and *piano*. At least I play them so.

Ex. 7

I find I have made no reference to the ten bars of piano introduction. Here is a sample of it.

Ex. 8   *Allegretto*

Bearing in mind that the *tempo* is quick the accompanist will find this quite a difficult moment for him. It needs practising. What is difficult about it? Playing the right notes, and playing them with a coquettish freedom.

It is often suggested that when really good English translations of Schubert, Schumann, or Brahms songs can be found it is desirable to use them when singing to an English-speaking audience. But surely if translations can be printed on the programme it is preferable to sing these songs in the language in which they were conceived since the German speech comes easily to an English tongue. Spanish pronunciation, however, is quite a problem to the Anglo-Saxon and translations are, so far as I know, non-existent. Are these songs then to be confined purely to Spanish singers? That fine artist Astra Desmond has shown us that this is not the case; she studied Spanish and its pronunciation and performed the songs of Spain with authenticity. Other singers may not have Miss Desmond's gift for languages or her intelligence, but they ought at least to strive to emulate her in devotion and musicianship. It is refreshing to stray occasionally off the beaten track.

Reprinted by permission of Union Musical Espagnola. Editors Carrera de San Jeronimo, 26, Madrid

G	E588	Hina Spani
O	RA184806	Ninon Vallin
P	R0324	Conchita Supervia (Frank Marshall)
V	16779	Gladys Swarthout (L. Lodges)
G	DA1976	Victoria de los Angeles (Gerald Moore)
V	1033	Lucrezia Bori
D	X10141	M. de los A. Morales (A. Dresden)
V	4464	C. Badia
C	DQ3462	A. Gimenez (A. Soresia)
V	4035	S. del Campo
C	RG16158	T. Robado (A. Romero)

THERE SCREECHED A BIRD

Translated from the
Norwegian of VILHELM KRAG
by ASTRA DESMOND

Music by EDVARD GRIEG
Op. 60 No. 4

IN 'Monsieur Croche the dilettante hater' (Noel Douglas) Claude Debussy, reviewing a Grieg concert in Paris, writes:

'At first I thought that I could only give colour impressions of Grieg's music. To begin with, the number of Norwegians who usually haunt the Colonne Concerts was tripled; we had never before been privileged to see so much red hair, or such extravagant hats—for the fashions in Christiania seem to me rather behind the times. Then the concert opened with a double turn: the performance of an overture called 'Autumn' and the ejection of a crowd of Grieg's admirers, who, at the bidding of a police constable, a slave to duty rather than to music, were sent to cool their enthusiasm on the banks of the Seine. Was a counter demonstration feared?

'It is not for me to say, but Grieg was in fact for a time the object of the most unappreciative comments; nor could I listen to his music just then, for I was busily engaged in coming to terms with several stern and splendid policemen.

'At last I saw Grieg. From in front he looks like a genial photographer; from behind his way of doing his hair makes him look like the plants called sunflowers, dear to parrots and the gardens that decorate small country stations. Despite his age, he is lean and vivacious and conducts the orchestra with care and vigour, stressing all the lights and shades and apportioning the expression with unflagging attention.

'It is a pity that Grieg's visit to Paris has taught us nothing new about his art; but he is an exquisite musician when he interprets the folk music of his country, although far from equalling Balakirev and Rimsky-Korsakov in the use they made of Russian folk music. Apart from this he is no more than a clever musician more concerned with effects than with genuine art.'

After reading this I have the impression, perhaps a mistaken one, that Debussy did not like Grieg.

Doubtless this article could be called entertaining journalism, though the malice in it reflects no credit on the author. As musical criticism it is not to be taken seriously. Yet the effect of such an attack must have been damaging in the extreme to Grieg's reputation, coming as it did from the leading French composer of the time. Where Debussy

91

—wielding an enormous influence—led, many followed. It is still fashionable today to dismiss Grieg with a shrug of the shoulders.

One hears of 'his flat rhythms—his lack of depth—his pretty little tunes'. But these criticisms, though applicable to some of his music, are far from true of all he wrote. Less than a dozen of the one hundred and forty songs he composed are heard in concert halls and these are by no means his best. For instance 'Jeg elsker Dig' (I love thee) and 'Solvejg's Song', though unmistakably Grieg, are not good measure of a composer who at his least was a splendid craftsman and at his best was capable of turning out a little masterpiece. But 'Der skreg en Fuhl' (There screeched a bird) is a finer song than either of these. How many people have ever heard of it? Precious few. It is not one of the pretty, pleasing popular ones and is never sung. Thanks to the industry and enthusiasm of Astra Desmond in unearthing, in studying, and performing many of these lesser known but more significant songs, their beauty is slowly percolating through to the consciousness of music lovers.

Miss Desmond, who has given me permission to use her excellent translation, says, in connexion with this song, 'Inside the cover of one of Grieg's pocket books, was found the motif with which this song begins and ends together with the words 'Gull's cry heard in Hardanger Fjord'.

Here is the *motif* in the pianoforte introduction and postlude, bars 1 to 6 and 21 to 26.

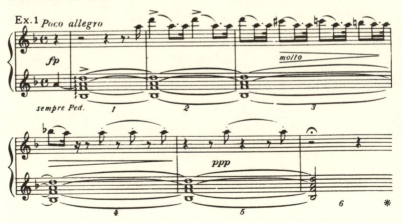

Throughout these six bars the same pedal is held. Each note of the first chord is played with great intensity (taking the top note with the right hand), while the screeches of the gull in the treble need a hard cruel touch which only yields to the *diminuendo*.

In all the examples I give—they cover the whole song—the expression marks are Grieg's. At the voice's entry he wants a much slower *tempo*. After the accent on 'screeched' the *crescendo* is a steep one with 'wide' its climax: these three beats (9) should be allowed plenty of time, plenty of space, in fact 'shoreless' describes it.

Ex. 2 *Lentamente*

There screeched a bird o'er the emp-ty sea, Wide and shore-less, it screeched with pain in the au-tumn gloom, Fluttered a bro-ken, weak, powerless wing,

The 'lame' figure in the bass from 11 to 16 is heavy, each movement from one octave to the next a painful one. In 13–14 the gull nearly comes to grief in those staggering fluttering triplets—his strength all but spent. There is an ominous silence in the voice part after 'broken' where the bird is falling, struggling. Effort, painful effort, must be manifest here.

The sinister and all-devouring grey sea, as exemplified by the threatening discords in the accompaniment, is the subject-matter of the singer's thoughts in the last phrase.

Ex. 3

Floa-ted on dus - ky pin-ions   Far ___ o'er the sea. ___

Strength is in that music, and the vocal line must be firm. As the song began, so it ends with the gull *motif* in the pianoforte. It is a bleak picture.

Peters Edition. Reprinted by permission of Hinrichsen Edition Ltd., London, W.C.1

D K962   Astra Desmond (Gerald Moore)

SLEEP

Poem by JOHN FLETCHER   *Music by* IVOR GURNEY

> Come, Sleep, and with thy sweet deceiving
> Lock me in delight awhile;
> Let some pleasing dreams beguile
> All my fancies, that from thence
> There may steal an influence,
> All my powers of care bereaving.
>
> Tho' but a shadow, but a sliding
> Let me know some little joy.
> We, that suffer long annoy
> Are contented with a thought
> Thro' an idle fancy wrought:
> O let my joys have some abiding.

COMPARING Gurney's setting of these words with the more popular setting by Peter Warlock, I have come to the conclusion that the poet would have preferred the Warlock song. There he would have found the peace that he craved. Sleep would have locked him in delight, bereaving him of care; he would have known some little joy, some short reprieve from his long annoy. The singer knows his appeal will be granted when he sings

Already the longed-for influence begins to steal over him during that descending line, and later the pianoforte's soft indeterminate discords tell of his benumbed senses

while that easeful major key of the final chord breathes sweet slumber.
  Since John Fletcher entitled his poem 'Sleep', one must assume that

95

the poem is rounded off with a sleep. It is for this reason, as I suggested, that the poet might have preferred Warlock's beautiful setting. But, naturally, I cannot be sure of this. Indeed my assumption may be wide of the mark, for did not Fletcher write

> There's nought in this life sweet,
> If man were wise to see't,
>   But only melancholy,
>   O sweetest melancholy.

It is therefore possible that he might have enjoyed the frustration inherent in the Gurney song.

On the whole I can be certain of one thing only; that Fletcher has heard neither of these settings and I boldly aver my preference for the Gurney, it is so deeply felt and so moving. 'Insomnia' might well have been the title for it. Here, the care and the long annoy are overpowering —inescapable. Here, 'O let my joys have some abiding' becomes a burning hunger, a passionate cry. It is entreaty, but agonized because vain.

The rocking figure in the accompaniment at the beginning could easily be disturbing.

This should not be allowed in the fairly tranquil first verse and can be obviated by using one pedal for each pair of semiquavers. A slight blurring of the harmonies will result from this treatment, but this does not matter provided the general level of tone be *pianissimo*. The composer's phrase marks must not cause the player to make conventional commas, pauses, or breaks in the flow of the music.

There is not one note in the voice part throughout which is not marked *legato*. The rests seen in bars 4 and 6 and in Example 2 should not be felt by the listener. They are put there to enable the singer to breathe, though he sings mentally even when he is making no sound: his concentration is never out of focus.

Very considerately the composer allows plenty of time for these breaths, but they must be taken quietly and without movement of face or body. Undeniably the phrases are long and present the singer with a formidable task, yet it is out of the question for him to breathe other than where a rest is marked. Were this poem read instead of sung no rests (as in 6 and 16) would be taken at all. This the singer must bear in mind.

While I am on the first verse let me point to the stresses on the first two semiquavers in 5; they give such expression to the word 'Sweet'. In making this word beautiful or in endeavouring to invest it with special meaning the singer must keep dead on the vocal line. I can best explain what I mean if I give a caricature of not keeping to the line.

Many artists with the best intentions would do this, thinking they were making 'sweet' more expressive. Again in 9–10 singers are taking away from the beauty of the music, not adding to it, if they slide from the B flat to the G, and from the C to the G, in this way:

The second verse is even more exacting than the first, for the phrases are longer and the feeling intensified.

Ex. 5

Both by the stresses in 26, 27 and by the *colla voce* the composer tells us how anxious he is that the performers should grasp the pitiful desperation of the words. In order to get the full measure of expression, this phrase can be taken as slow as the singer likes, each note dwelt on, the *tempo* being resumed by the pianist on the word 'joy'. The singer's yearning is answered on the pianoforte by a stress on the third beat of 28.

This yearning reaches its highest peak, as I said earlier, in 35 to 37 and 38 to 41. I give these two phrases in full in Example 6; they are the very essence of Gurney's conception of the poem—pain and a disquieted spirit. If the reader will refer to my first quotation from the Warlock song he will see the fundamental difference between the two settings.

Provided he keeps meticulously to his *legato* line the singer need exercise no restraint on, to be literal, the outburst in 35–36. This is the

consummation of his anguish. Once again I caution against the tendency—particularly if the singer be affected by the emotion in the
words and music—to slur.

It is strange that the composer, having phrase-marked every note
of the vocal line, should omit to do so over the last four notes. I feel
that he would have liked one long phrase-line from 38 to 42 but
refrained from making what he must have felt was an unreasonable
demand. It is a cruel test to have to sing all this without an intervening
breath—but that is the way to do it. I have only heard John Coates
do this and I do not want to hear it done in any other way: it is white
hot. A heavy emotion-laden *crescendo* from 'have' (39) up to 'some'—

for which the composer asks—precludes any idea of a breath. This phrase is no whit less intense than the preceding one (35 to 37) and a breath lets in an unwanted draught of coolness, an ease which the emotion of the music belies.

Pangs which match his own will be heard by the singer in the accompanist's chords in 36, in the chromatic descent in 37-38, and finally in the postlude's weariness in 43-44. Even the chord of B flat major at the end sounds a note of interrogation.

Ex. 7

Reprinted by permission of Boosey & Hawkes Ltd., (Excerpts from Warlock's 'Sleep' reprinted by permission of Oxford University Press)

OFFRANDE

Words by PAUL VERLAINE   *Music by* REYNALDO HAHN

THIS poem under the title 'Green' has been set to music by Claude Debussy and Gabriel Fauré, and no doubt both their settings are of greater worth than the one I propose to discuss: Debussy's scintillates with freshness and with the sparkle of early morning dew

and Fauré's speaks from fullness of heart with the ring of true devotion.

We are invigorated after performing or hearing the first song, we are moved by the second. I love them both. Why then, have I chosen Reynaldo Hahn's setting for inclusion here? Because I am intrigued by it, and because this composer's songs should be heard more often.

Beneath a frigid exterior this song is passionate and sensuous. Its calm expression is deceptive so that we are almost unaware of the hunger which it masks, of the longing surging through its veins.

Debussy's buoyant 'Ne le déchirez pas avec vos deux mains blanches' is rhetorical. It wears a confident smile proclaiming a conquest won.

But in this very phrase Hahn conveys a sense of frustration; compare his handling of it (7–8) with the above example:

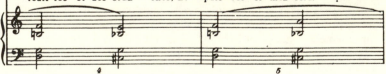

Whereas Debussy's soars gracefully without a hint of misgiving, here the voice steps down note by note an entire octave so that at the words 'l'humble présent' the eyes of the supplicant have dropped in self-abasement. It is a supplication, we fear, that may well be disregarded, the lover's heart easily bruised. Each bar is pregnant with entreaty and, although it is nearly all sung very softly, suggests an undercurrent of passion. Young lover's shyness marks the singer's first words so that the quaver rest in 2 is slightly lengthened, making 'Voici des fruits' a quickened utterance; after a lengthened quaver rest 'des fleurs' is quickly said again, and so too 'des feuilles et des branches'.

The grouping of these phrases is intentionally spasmodic and yet it is all intimately uttered, albeit the diction is fresh and clear and the *legato* never lost. Perhaps it is not until bar 5 that we first become aware of the song's basic *tempo*, for the slight suggestion of breathlessness at the beginning here gives way to a calm control: marked *très doux* 'Voici mon cœur', &c., should be imbued with intense feeling.

There is no doubting the physical and mental fatigue in the following example:

Ex. 2

Souf - frez que ma fa - ti-gue, à vos pieds re - po - sé - e,

Rè - ve des chers in - stants ___ qui la dé - las - se - ront ___

Nor can 'Rêve des chers instants' be anything but hopeless and anaemic when placed beside Fauré's full-blooded embrace.

The song ends with an unresolved discord on the pianoforte.

Ex. 3

What will be the outcome?

Reynaldo Hahn was undoubtedly a lightweight but he was a charming writer and I wish singers would give his songs an occasional airing. His name often figures on the programmes of such consummate artists as Maggie Teyte and Jennie Tourel, which is sufficient recommendation.

Reprinted by permission of Editions Musicales Andre Gregh, Suc[r], Paris

G   DA1201   Vanni-Marcoux (Piero Coppola)
O   188766   Roger Bourdin
Pat X93137   Jean Planel
G   DA1821   Maggie Teyte (Gerald Moore)
G   P371   Reynaldo Hahn (self-acc.)
L   3.00.011 M. Hamel (J. Ullern)

SHE NEVER TOLD HER LOVE

Words by SHAKESPEARE   *Music by* HAYDN

THIS noble song begins with a fourteen-bar pianoforte introduction
which must be played with infinite breadth and dignity. The accompanist has complete confidence in his ability to play this opening with
controlled strength and tenderness: this confidence enables him to obey
Haydn's instruction *Largo assai, e con espressione*, for he knows that by
playing it sufficiently slowly he will have the ample time needed in 5,
for instance, for the *piano* to sound clearly after the *sforzando*; for the
curve at 11 to have a special beauty.

It is most important that every rest be observed, the pedal is not
used at all from 2 to 5 nor from 12 to 14. These detached chords give

the music a remarkable significance and it would be the greatest mistake to run them together with the sustaining pedal. In two places, I feel, a very slight use of *rubato* is permitted: the two quavers on the fourth beat of 6 should be dwelt on, and the fourth beat of 11 should not be passed over with too meticulous a regard for exact *tempo*.

The song really begins at bar 2 and I have never understood why Haydn wanted that tonic chord in bar 1; however, there it is and we have to play it. I play it as marked with a *fermata* but I make a distinct break before embarking on the stately rhythm of bar 2.

Of course the singer is just as interested in the introduction as is her partner, she wants to hear the *tempo* established which (agreed upon in rehearsal) will enable her to contain each vocal phrase in one breath, without discomfort. She hopes it will not be necessary at 15 to alter the *tempo* in any way. She listens to this introduction and, like the audience, becomes absorbed in the atmosphere. If it is beautifully played she is inspired.

Ex. 2

These phrases look deceptively short, and indeed they seem short to everybody except the singer. Owing to the slow movement of the song they are quite long to sing and need the firmest breath control. 'Love' on 16 and 18 coming at the end of each phrase is difficult to keep steady in view of the fact that it is less in weight than 'never told', but it must be pure and the listener is disturbed if pressure is brought to bear on it.

Above all the singer keeps her smooth line unsullied by any *portamenti* or slurs; she is as particular about this as Casals would be in the slow movement of a Bach suite. Where an entire song is as completely *legato* as this, the singer must listen intently to every note she sings, for this sliding is insidious and the most conscientious of artists can be unaware they are doing it. I have seen utter astonishment on a lady's face when I have told her that she was sliding from one note to another at 29 (fourth beat), 31, 35. It will be seen that these three bars (29, 31, 35) have one thing in common, namely, each is a falling progression.

The last two notes of the second beat of 32 come into the same category; these semiquavers are lingered on.

Two more eloquent opportunities for the accompanist occur at 24 to 26 and 33, 34. I give one of these instances with Haydn's markings and in parenthesis my own, in an endeavour to show how a delicate—but a delicate—*rubato* may be employed.

The turns on the first and third beats of 26 are done with all the leisure possible.

I have alluded several times to the third beat here, the fourth beat there; this was done for convenience. In reality and despite the song's slow and stately march, singer and partner should feel only two beats to the bar.

'She never told her love' takes nearly three and a half minutes to perform.

Published by Augener Ltd.

G	DA1850	Elisabeth Schumann (Gerald Moore)
G	EC174	Marian Anderson (Franz Rupp)
ALLO	AL13	E. Rogers (E. Mitrani)
V	26707	M. Houston (Frank la Forge)

SEA FEVER

Words by JOHN MASEFIELD   *Music by* JOHN IRELAND

I ONCE asked John Ireland which of the many songs he had written he considered his best, and he replied without hesitation 'Sea Fever'. Bearing in mind that many of his other lovely songs (which must have cost him much labour, time, and reflection) are more complicated and more difficult to perform, I thought his answer extremely instructive.

The great virtue of this setting lies in the fact that the music, though bearing the unmistakable stamp of the composer's individuality, never imprisons the words. If you were reciting this poem, your rhythm by and large would be the same as Ireland's vocal line.

It is wise when studying this song to recite the words, and after that to put the same speech-rhythm into your singing, for no composer, John Ireland or anyone else, can possibly put on the printed page the delicate divergence from strict *tempo* that such a song as this requires.

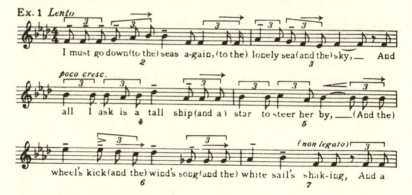

Try, for argument's sake, singing these bars in the most rigid *tempo*. Give the three quavers on each beat the same strength and the same weight, and you will find that the words and the music have lost impetus, life, and meaning. The music was expressly designed here to give the words free play; the singer of imagination employs *tempo rubato*. Any detailed discussion of *rubato* is dangerous in that, trying to bring his point home, the demonstrator is apt to exaggerate, and this puts a spotlight at once on something which should be a secret and delicate affair. I must content myself, rather than inflict on the reader a description of the entire song bar by bar, by indicating here and there the sort of *rubato* I would employ if I were a singer.

In Example 1 for instance, the stresses show which notes (or rather words) require more weight and time, the parentheses and arrows indicate words needing less weight and which should be hastened. The second verse has a more impatient temper and bars 12 to 14 could be taken in this style:

A sentence where the singer's sibilants make the picture very real is 'and the flung spray and the blown spume, and the seagulls crying'.

After the deliberation of the first verse and the impatience of the second, Roy Henderson started the third verse with an intensity which was tautened by a slight lessening of tone, a reduction which made the huge *crescendo* up to 'where the wind's like a whetted knife' all the fiercer.

The even quavers in bar 25 should be noticed.

In contrast to the *legato* of bar 24, these quavers are decidedly *non legato* so that you can really fancy the man laughing; and the *tempo* here is slightly broadened to give effect to this only bar of even quavers in the whole song. 'Merry' is hardly a triplet, one gets as quickly as possible on to the second syllable.

These little suggestions of give and take in the rhythm—all without disturbing the song's basic *tempo*—are prompted by my recollection of Roy Henderson's interpretation (with which I was in complete accord) but they are, I repeat, suggestions. I am not laying down hard and fast rules that this note must be hurried and that note held, but I do insist that some sort of elasticity, flexibility, *rubato*, or whatever you like to call it, must be employed according to individual taste.

One word of warning to the singer is necessary—he must be certain he pitches his long note in bar 27 high enough.

Ex. 4

qui - et sleep and a sweet dream when the long trick's o - ver.
        26   27   28

There is a tendency after 'quiet sleep and a sweet dream' for the performer to relax. I have often heard this happen. Certainly the mood is now relaxed and the tone soft, but the singer does not lose concentration or forget the breath support this note needs, otherwise he will flatten it.

There are not many male singers, amateur or professional, who have not got a copy of 'Sea Fever' lying somewhere near the piano, and the reason for this is not far to seek. The words are superb and the music is perfectly wedded to them; moreover every man feels better for having sung it.

Reprinted by permission of Augener Ltd.

G B2594	Stuart Robertson (Gerald Moore)
V 1583	Conrad Thibault
G B9073	Robert Irwin (Gerald Moore)
G E553	John Brownlee
G E3	Fraser Gange
G B9257	Paul Robeson
G B10233	Frederick Harvey
G M526	Roy Henderson (Ivor Newton)

FRÜHLINGSLIED

Words in Swabian dialect   *Music by* MENDELSSOHN

'AUF Flügeln des Gesanges' (On Wings of Song) was not the only song Mendelssohn wrote, yet it is the only one we ever hear. This composer does not seize you by the throat, he does not soar to the heights nor plumb the depths, but Elisabeth Schumann always delighted her audiences with Mendelssohn songs (or anybody's songs for that matter!). They take you into a fairyland of soft airs and graces. I wish singers, women especially, would give them a little attention, for their innocent Victorian charm would not come amiss in these days. 'Bei der Wiege' (Cradle Song), quite Schubertian in style; 'Wenn durch die Piazzetta' (Venetian Song), a tender melodic setting so different from Schumann's; 'Hexenlied' (Witches Song), an exciting affair not unworthy of Loewe; 'Neue Liebe' (New Love), with its fairies from *Midsummer Night's Dream*; all these and others would amply repay study.

'Frühlingslied' simply tells us that spring has come with its blue sky, warm breezes, twittering birds, and budding trees.

Like some of the songs mentioned above, it has an accompaniment that plays a lively part. It supplies more than a demure background such as we find in 'Wings of Song' and its introduction, fresh and crisp, gives us a taste of the sparkle that is to come.

Ex. 1 *Allegretto*

From the first note the player makes it obvious that he is really enjoying himself. He makes 1, 2, 3, 5, 7 *legato* as marked, but in 4 and 6 he plays the *staccato* repeated note with relish, trying to lift his hands as high as he can off the keys between each note; these bars bounce.

III

So keen is the singer to impart zest to her part and clarity to her words that it matters not at all if she sings *non legato*. In fact the dainty tripping rhythm of the movement dictates this. Only at 10 and 15, and in parallel instances, will she be able to give us a moment's *cantabile*.

Ex. 2

Jetzt kommt der   Früh - ling, der Him-mel isch   blau, ____

At 22, 23 and 42, 43 and 63, 64 the phrases will be more graceful and a perfect fusion between voice and piano made easier if the singer makes a slight *rallentando*. No singer will object to this, for her semiquavers really must be *legato* here.

Ex. 3

die Lüf-te-gen lau,   jetzt ____ kommt der Früh - ling!

Her little *cadenza* at the end of the third verse can, of course, be *a piàcere* (and she can make as much of the three pauses as she pleases), it is a graceful little flourish to adorn her departure from the scene.

Ex. 4

ein   Vei - - 66 - - - - - - 67 ge-le strauss.

In the accompaniment to the second verse, the birds chirrup and trill,

Ex. 5

Jetzt kommt der   Früh - ling,

die Vög-le im Wald _____ zwit _____ schern und
lo-cka ih-re Wei-ble wol bald

while in the postlude 68 to 77 we hear a cuckoo calling; he is joined by his mate at 74.

Ex. 6

Published by Boosey & Hawkes L:d.

ALLO AL51   Elisabeth Schumann (George Schick)

THE EVENING PRAYER

English translation by   *Words and Music by*

E. M. LOCKWOOD   M. MOUSSORGSKY

THE seven songs known as 'Songs of Childhood' express in terms of words and music the amusing and extraordinary twists and turns of a child's mind. This set is a work of genius. Moussorgsky gives us the psychology of a child as surely as he reveals the psychology of 'Boris Godounoff' or 'Ivan the Terrible'. 'Evening Prayer' in common with the other songs in this set is couched in childish language which, by its very nature, precludes any prima donna-ish approach. The diva, in an impressive creation with train attached, with tiara, with long kid gloves, cannot sing this song with the same regal mien as she sings Beethoven's 'Die Ehre Gottes aus der Natur'. This is not to imply that she should take off her bejewelled trappings and appear on the platform in diapers: it simply means that the song should be sung as a child would sing it. Irmgard Seefried, elegant and sophisticated though she is, sings this song with delicious naïveté, and Oda Slobotskaya reduced her brilliant and thrilling voice to a childish treble in her amusing characterization.

In the first place then, it requires a soprano who can, at will, reduce her voice to the dimensions of a piping little treble; secondly it requires an artist who is something of an actress. (Every serious concert singer of any distinction acts. He is so utterly living in the song that the expression on his face is bound to reflect the mood or the character of the music. In 'Erlkönig' the parts of the terrified boy, the anxious father, the threatening Erlking cannot each be delivered with the same wooden countenance; the singer in turn looks terrified, anxious, threatening. The singer caught up in the religious ecstasy of 'Die junge Nonne' seems to us to be a different person when she sings 'Das Köhlerweib ist trunken'. But when I say a good singer acts I do not mean for one moment that gestures are desirable. Far from it. Chaliapin, great actor as he was on the operatic stage, never stepped outside the framework of the song on the concert platform. A calculated step forward here, a fluttering movement of the hands there, are distracting to the audience. Gestures are barred. Everything is concentrated into the voice, and the singer with heart, brain, temperament, and love of what he is singing will find that his face reflects his thoughts. And this is the only outward and visible sign that is needed.)

Kneeling in his cot, with his nurse ready to prompt him, the little chap starts confidently:

Ex. 1 *Allegro moderato*

> Bless, O Lord I pray Thee, Dad - dy and Mum - my,
> Bless them and take care of them!

But it is so difficult to concentrate when one is tired and already, at bar 5, his thoughts are beginning to wander. The *fermata* at the end of this bar comes quite abruptly—there is an awkward silence while nurse wills the child to continue. This hesitation continues for the first sixteen bars of the song while Brother Vasenka and Brother Mishenka and darling old Grandmamma are remembered. Then the excitement really starts with an alarming catalogue of uncles and aunts, cousins and play-mates, all tumbling over one another in profusion. From 17 to 27 is a gradual *crescendo* with an *accelerando* thrown in at 25. 'Auntie Katie, Auntie Natasha, Auntie Masha, Auntie Paresha, Aunties Lionba Varia and Sasha and Olia, and Tania and Nadia. Uncles Petia and Kolia, Volodia and Grisha and Sasha', &c. &c. &c. The singer becomes more breathless as the music loudens and quickens.

At 24, 25, 26 the climax is reached and here Moussorgsky's accom-paniment is so unpianistic that I suggest the following simpler but equally effective alternative for the left hand.

Ex. 2

'Nanny, dear Nanny, now what else?' asks the child, and the nurse replies

Ex. 3

> You really are a lit-tle monkey!   How many times I've

Growing impatience on the nurse's part is shown by the loudening and reiterated G's in the accompaniment at 31, while the repeated chord in 33 suggests a little slap on the wrist. Many a singer misses Moussorgsky's instruction at 34. The *forte* sign is significant. The humourless nurse is quite incapable of appreciating that her little five-year-old charge can scarcely be guilty of wickedness—a little naughtiness at the most but not wickedness. Therefore she sings 'Pardon I beseech thee Lord, all my wickedness' in almost a stentorian voice and with the sternest expression. Therein lies the humour. One feels that if there are policewomen in heaven, this nurse will be a sergeant in the force.

Echoing the nurse's words in the meekest and tiniest voice, the little innocent concludes the song with

Before the singer has finished her triplet in 39 the pianist's chord is released so that the word 'Nanny' is left alone in mid-air.

Reprinted by permission of Augener Ltd.

C 17312D   Nelson Eddy

TAKE, O TAKE THOSE LIPS AWAY

('*Measure for Measure*')

Words by SHAKESPEARE   *Music by* C. HUBERT PARRY

I LAST played this song for John Coates in 1926, since when I have never heard it performed. I am at a loss to account for this as, in my opinion, the song is a fine one and worthy of inclusion in recital programmes.

Singer and pianist must make up their minds if they are going to tackle this song to do it as Parry wanted it done, dramatically. They do not treat nuances in a wishy-washy manner, they storm them full-bloodedly, with sharp rises and falls of tone, so that a *crescendo* comes on you so suddenly and vividly that for a moment you are scorched by the heat and then as quickly cooled, as if you had opened the door of a furnace and straightway closed it again. In this way the listener will be gripped by the throat. This song is too violent for any gentler treatment.

A feature worthy of remark is the false accent on the half beat so clearly seen in the introductory bars, and obtaining generally throughout the song in the piano part; a rhythmical device that seems to give an undercurrent of poignancy to the singer's declamation.

Ex. 1 *Lento*

This introduction is played with intensity, with a continual *crescendo* up to the first beat on 4, and the pianist's aim, it seems to me, should not be to describe a succession of graceful curves executed with a relaxed wrist; on the contrary the line is angular, and the tone quality produced by unyielding fingers and wrist is hard. It should be remembered however that the stark nature of the sound desired does not necessarily call for an unceasing *forte*, by which the singer would be drowned. One can dig a hard tone out of the pianoforte without having to employ a sledgehammer.

In his very first phrase the singer makes us feel his desperation. It will help him to imbue his tone with bitterness if he frowns, for a smile on his lips would be as much out of place as a soothing quality of sound: he is not pleading, he is censuring.

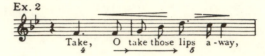

Ex. 2

I have marked the three passing quavers with an arrow to indicate that after the first 'Take' the singer hastens up to 'lips' on which he lingers as long as he dares; so long, in fact, that he is forced to shorten the first syllable of 'away'. This roughly is the shape of the *rubato* which should be employed in 9, 10, 11 where we make a *fermata* on 'lights', and then hurry the passing notes in order to give more time again on the dotted quaver of 'mislead'.

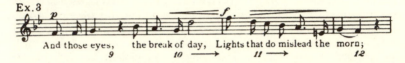

Ex. 3

If the singer can possibly do the whole phrase from the crotchet rest of 9 to bar 12 in one breath, it will be wonderful; if not, I ask him to consider seriously the idea of breathing after the word 'lights' rather than before it, for the effect of the *crescendo* on 'day' being carried without break up to 'lights' is quite electrifying.

Only at 13–14 does the music seem to lapse into tenderness as if resolution had weakened

Ex. 4

and here the pianist suggests the change of mood and gives the singer time for it by introducing the *pianissimo* chord with utmost deliberation. This weakening, if indeed it be such, is momentary for once again we are storming up to a climax on 'seals of love' (a high *tenuto* note for the singer—a crashing bass for the pianist)—to be followed by the most bitter phrase 20, 21, 22 of the whole song:

Ex. 5

Those three notes in the vocal part need thinking about. In the first place the singer takes care that the *piano* is not too soft and then he makes a big *crescendo* on his 'Seal'd' which is joined without any break on to the next note an octave lower, and finally he attacks the G flat on 'vain' with energy and venom before the tone fades. Breath must be regulated, for there is a *ritardando* going on and of course these three notes must be relentlessly joined together. The accompanist does what he can to help by playing 19 and 20 with intensity and he makes sure that we hear the singer's G flat echoed in the last bar of the pianoforte.

Reprinted by permission of Novello & Co. Ltd.

BLOW, BLOW, THOU WINTER WIND

Words by SHAKESPEARE   *Music by* ROGER QUILTER
                                                    Op. 6 No. 3

IN his book entitled *French Music* (published by Oxford University Press) Martin Cooper suggests that an equivalent figure in English music to Reynaldo Hahn might be Roger Quilter. This comparison, I think, is extraordinarily apt. When one considers Mr. Cooper's comments on Hahn's compositions '. . . precise and finished workmanship, a nice adjustment of means to ends . . . a preference for clear and thin texture . . . [Hahn] combines an elegant musicianship with a pretty wit and a gift for charmingly nostalgic melody . . .' it will readily be agreed that the composer under discussion might well be Quilter.

'To Daisies', 'Dream Valley', 'Go Lovely Rose', 'Now Sleeps the Crimson Petal', are all gentle in mood and movement and the words demand lyrical, nostalgic, refined music to do them justice. Roger Quilter has set them once and for all. But could one say the same of 'Blow, Blow, Thou Winter Wind'? Do the kindly charm of his music and the elegance of his style, qualities so desirable in Herrick, Blake, &c., for which we are so grateful, stand in his way in a song of such bitterness as this?

It all depends on the singer and the accompanist.

I have nevertheless chosen this song because it presents the performers with an interesting problem, namely how to infuse into the musical setting the toughness and the cynicism that the words demand. The accompanist can help a great deal to sharpen the edges but it is mostly the singer's responsibility. Time after time one has heard tenors bleat, and with the suavest *legato* line—to say nothing of the blandest of smiles —the following:

Ex. 1 *Poco più allegro*

120

Is it that after having been in the minor mode for the first section singers feel they can settle down snugly and comfortably now that they are in the major? The words give the lie to this. And why *legato*, when the composer does not ask for it? Bars 18 and 19 with their aspirates should be sung frankly with no attempt to achieve an impossible joining of one note to another. Again, the initial consonant of 'friendship'—'feigning' —'Folly' should be in each case violently projected to make Shakespeare's alliteration patent to the listener and to enable the singer to pour all the scorn into the words he possibly can.

'Loving' is another word where the first consonant is stressed, but here after allowing the 'l' to curl angrily round the tongue, the rest of the word must be thrown away. There is all the difference in the world between the rhythm and meaning of the word here and the caressing of it in, for example, Purcell's duet 'My Dearest, My Fairest'

or the tenderness of it in Maud Valérie White's 'So We'll Go No More a-Roving'.

All these stresses that I enjoin take time, be it understood, and the accompanist fashions his playing accordingly. In the piano part there are spikes in the *staccato* chords of 20–21. The semiquavers in 21–22–23 are like the crack of a whip; there should be a slight *rubato* with them, their entry being delayed, a delay which forces the player to flick them quickly in order to get to the fourth quaver of the bar *in time*. I recommend that most of the semiquavers in the pianoforte part be treated in this way, in bars 10 and 12 for example, and 33 to 37; the commas in

Example 1 are inserted by me to show my meaning. The pianist was asked earlier to 'wait on' the singer for the liberties the latter takes with his *rubato*, and clearly it is the singer's duty here to do the same service for his partner.

At the end of the chorus it is essential that the singer obeys the composer's *crescendo* on 'jolly'.

Ex. 2

this life ___ is ___ most jol - ly.
        29   30   31   32

There can be no doubt that the second syllable is stronger than the first in this instance, and the note is released abruptly thus giving an air of desperation or disgust to the situation; for what the singer is saying in effect is 'This life is most jolly. *I don't think!*'

The song begins impressively.

Ex. 3   *Non troppo allegro ma vigoroso e con moto*

If the pianist plays his preliminary chords with *brio* it will give the singer the support he needs to attack his 'Blow, blow' with courage. This opening is full of gusto and the G flat should be startling for there is nothing in bars 1 and 2 to indicate that we are in the minor key.

Personally I hate to hear 'winter wind' rhyming with 'so unkind', the vowel in 'wind' should be as in 'tin' or 'win': it would be just as logical to make 'warp' rhyme with 'sharp'. The singer, however, must decide this question for himself.

Reprinted by permission of Boosey & Hawkes Ltd. (Excerpt from Maude Valérie White's 'So We'll Go No More a-Roving' reprinted by permission of Chappell & Co. Ltd.)

        G B2500   George Baker
        G B4379   Derek Oldham
        C 4817   Frank Mullings
        D F2062   Henry Wendon
        C L1055   Gervase Elwes (Frederick Kiddle)

SPRING WATERS

Words *by* FEODOR TIOUTCHEV   Music *by* S. RACHMANINOFF
English version by ROSA NEWMARCH   *Op. 14 No. 11*

ALTHOUGH I am not particularly fond of this song, I want to write a little about the accompaniment. Sopranos like to sing 'Spring Waters' occasionally because it makes a climax at the end of a group with its gusto, top notes, and dashing accompaniment. In fact it is a song popular with everyone except, perhaps, the average accompanist. He finds some of the technical passages extremely difficult taken at top speed, and some of the large chords beyond his compass. Rachmaninoff in his piano writing did not take lesser mortals into account, and with his own enormous stretch had no difficulty whatsoever in crashing down on chords like

and

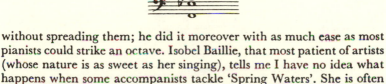

without spreading them; he did it moreover with as much ease as most pianists could strike an octave. Isobel Baillie, that most patient of artists (whose nature is as sweet as her singing), tells me I have no idea what happens when some accompanists tackle 'Spring Waters'. She is often afraid to put it on the programme. I have heard other singers say the same.

From the very first bar the accompaniment suggests the surging of the waters. Geographically the first seven bars are pretty much alike, so it behoves the pianist to make up his mind what fingering he is going to use and having made up his mind, to stick to it.

The second beat of the bar which I have fingered is the only difficulty here. Of course the sustaining pedal is used—there would be no surge without it, but that does not mean that all the semiquavers should be unclean. So, after practising my method of playing it as shown in Example 1, let those accompanists who find they are still unsure try this fingering which can also be applied to bars 2, 3, 4, 6, and 7

It is, however, when the singer says, 'The banks are sunny where they flow' that the accompanist's sky is clouded over and his pianistic flow congealed. And at the words 'They sparkle as they run more clear', the playing sounds more muddy and obscure than ever. This occurs at bars 8 and 10. Remembering that the song goes like the wind, it was marvellous with what ease Rachmaninoff 'threw away' those passages when playing them. He wrote them as follows:

To give the pianist an added interest in the proceedings, the passages are not quite alike. They are great stumbling blocks for him. Above these rushing semiquavers, the singer has a soaring phrase and she will storm up this phrase without paying any heed to the accompanist's difficulties. And rightly. So joyous is the mood that she wants to sweep the audience along with her in her enthusiasm; she has no time to wait about for a stumbling accompanist. The latter must give the impression that he overcomes these technical difficulties with the greatest ease. I do not mean by this that he should 'show off' but I do recommend that he tries not to make it too obvious that he is in travail. By crouching ferociously over the keyboard with clenched teeth, he will hardly look, from the audience's viewpoint, as if he is enjoying himself. Therefore I suggest to those who cannot cover bars 8 and 10 easily, the following simpler alternatives:

On the first two beats of 20 and 21,

my arrangement of the chords is thinner than the original but easier to play at the very fast *tempo* required here. In any case the composer uses exactly the same positioning of the chords in 15 and 16. A tremendous accent on the bass octave—with sustaining pedal—helps here too. And at 35 in the left hand instead of Rachmaninoff's

I suggest

which will be much easier.

Let me warn the pianist that there are one or two places where he can easily drown the singer unless he constantly keeps his eye on the vocal line. At bars 5 and 6, for instance, the *tessitura* is quite low, especially if the singer is able to take the low B flat which Rachmaninoff preferred.

The rush-ing of spring floods draws near _____

Here is an example where the voice part is marked *forte* but where the accompanist's *forte* must be discreet. Where the singer is taking a top note or where she is silent, the accompanist can always make a surging *crescendo* provided he is prepared to damp down his tone equally quickly when it is necessary.

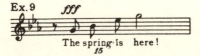

The spring is here!

At 15 the voice and pianoforte are marked *fff* and it should be instinctive on the accompanist's part to be merciful on the first half of the bar. He can louden hugely on the top note.

I must apologize to the singer if I appear to have given all my attention in 'Spring Waters' to the accompanist. It is not that I wish to belittle the singer for in this instance she has more responsibility to carry than her partner; her brilliance and her verve are the most important factors in the song's success. The man at the piano, however, can easily be too overpowering or, what is worse, too stagnant.

My advice may, in the long run, not only contribute towards a successful performance of the song but may also help to preserve a desirable spirit of amity between singer and accompanist. Too often the soprano walks off the stage at the conclusion of 'Spring Waters' nourishing hatred for her colleague in her bosom. It is much nicer to be on speaking terms, and that is up to the accompanist.

Reprinted by permission of Boosey & Hawkes Ltd.

G	ER289	Ada Sari
C	LX1038	Jennie Tourel (Erich Itor Kahn)
D	M602	Marjorie Lawrence (Ivor Newton)
Voc	B3104	Vladimir Rosing (Frank St. Leger)
V	4548	D. Dickson
P	R20378	Vladimir Rosing (H. Gellhorn)

CHANSON À BOIRE

Words by PAUL MORAND   *Music by* MAURICE RAVEL

RAVEL's three songs which comprise the set known as 'Don Quichotte à Dulcinée' can be performed separately, and I have chosen the drinking song for inclusion here because tenors and baritones are constantly asking for a brilliant song with which to end a group. Nobody likes to walk off the platform to the sound of his own footsteps and it is perhaps natural that a singer wants to wind up proceedings with a song that is bound to provoke applause as I said in 'Spring Waters'.

The high-pitched vocal line and the continuous *forte* combine to make 'Chanson à boire' strenuous for the singer, yet he appears to sing with careless abandon for he is in high good humour: the whole thing is a tipsy and rowdy affair.

It will be seen by my illustrations, which are in the tenor key, how high is the *tessitura*.

Also, be it observed, the line is *legato*. It would be far easier to accentuate each note in a *non legato* way: and the same applies here:

But a *staccato* here would sound absurd. It is no easy task to execute the above example smoothly and to avoid an intrusive 'h', yet the idea behind the desire for *legato* is logical. Imagine a man stretched out comfortably in a chair, glass in hand, sufficiently inebriated to be in a most optimistic frame of mind; he would disdain to sing *staccato*, in fact such singing would require an energetic use of the diaphragm that, in his recumbent attitude, he is in no position to fulfil. (To complete the picture attendant on the consequences of such vocal explosiveness, I feel impelled to add that there would be danger, tragic under the circumstances, of spilling some precious drops of wine.)

It will be seen at 30 and at 31 that our hero has nearly two bars rest, here he clambers to his feet and drinks; his utterances at 32,

and from bar 39 to the end of the verse, become much more energetic and disjointed.

Ravel has marked a heavy slur at 32 with a really short quaver for the word 'bois', and he gives us a hiccup from the pianoforte at 40. The laughter from 43 to 46 (anticipated when Pierre Bernac sings it by a chuckle at 41, 42) requires some consideration. Paul Morand's verse reads 'Ah! Ah! Ah!' and Ravel has naturally written this on his score, but for singing purposes 'Ha! Ha! Ha!' is preferable with as much intrusive 'h' as you please—and this is the way Pierre Bernac does it, so far as I recall. At all events I recommend this slight alteration as being more suggestive of laughter. 'Joie' on the first beat of 44 and 46 has been marked with an *apportamento*, but the effect wanted is not a slow slide from the lower note to the upper for that would take too long and would pull the rhythm to pieces: it is merely that the high E is attacked from underneath so that the vowel is heard before the voice has reached the E. In the discussion of Ivor Gurney's 'Sleep' I attempted to expose a bad singer's habit of breaking a clean vowel line by this very thing that Ravel wants. Here we consciously commit this offence for it is a special effect absolutely in character and would, I think, best be illustrated thus:

Ex. 5

so that the 'j' of 'joie' is tacked on to the 'la'. This robs 'la' but enables the first beat of 44 and 46 to be attacked on time.

There are no problems for the accompanist except in the first bars of his introduction, which are terrifying.

Ex. 6 *Allegro* ($\bullet$ = 184)

Played slowly there is no difficulty at all, but alas, the *tempo* is a fast one. The chords in the right hand would not be unreasonable to contain, were it not for the rude intrusion of the left hand which persists in getting in the way. I admit that I found it very exasperating and awkward to play this and the corresponding passages at 51 to 53 and 103 to 105 with rapidity and accuracy until Bernac came to my rescue by telling me that any notes in the left hand will do. The composer played the right-hand chords as written, and even then the first chord of each bar was his chief concern; but his left hand was slapped down on any bunch of notes provided they were in the vicinity of those indicated. Ravel wanted the effect of a clattering noise such as a big man would make falling or stumbling into his chair.

Shall we say in the final bars that the wine-bibber rolls off his chair to the floor with a bump?

Ex. 7

Reprinted by permission of Messrs. Durand et Cie.

G   DA4865   Martial Singher
G   DA1869   Pierre Bernac (Francis Poulenc)
BaM 32   Yvon le Marc Hadour (Mme le Marc Hadour)
D   LXT2568   Gérard Souzay

D'ANNE JOUANT DE L'ESPINETTE

Words by CLEMENT MAROT   *Music by* MAURICE RAVEL

IT is not the simplest thing in the world to make a modern concert grand
pianoforte sound like a spinet, but Ravel has made this accompaniment
so fragile and arranged its *tessitura* so cleverly that it is not too impossible
to create the illusion. I once heard it proposed that a spinet should be
used for the performance of this song. Nothing could be further from
Ravel's mind than this; nothing could be more horribly boring. Our
pianoforte of today is capable of such a wide variety of colour that it
is really great fun to try to make it sound like the instrument of old,
moreover there is a hint of richness and warmth needed that no spinet
could impart. Only the use of the sustaining pedal, which some of the
legato phrases demand, can give this colour. 'Très doux' is the label for
the voice part; prominent though the accompaniment is, it must always
be gentle with the soft pedal depressed all the time: 'En sourdine' says
Ravel.

Ex. 1   *Très léger et d'un rythme précis*

We try to make the semiquavers *staccato*, but sometimes the necessity for the melodic rise and fall must override this consideration; see 3, 4, 5, 6. It would be impossible to fulfil Ravel's *legato* signs without judicious use of the pedal—even the dear little inflexions at 6 would be dry without it. As for the last beat of 6 the pedal seems to catch only the faintest echo of those four notes because they are so delicately touched; they can just be heard under the chord, high up in the treble at 7. This chord surely has been written for the left hand in preference to the right to give the impression that it is plucked like a harp-string. I think of a harp, pluck the chord, then throw my hand in the air.

Almost like an *obligato* the voice enters an octave lower than the piano which now repeats, more or less, its introductory pattern. The singer is in no danger of being submerged by the accompaniment, for his line must invariably be sung *legato*.

He would be greatly mistaken were he to make all the semiquavers 'détaché', anybody could sing them that way. To be sure, they are fairly rapid and delivered with sharp diction; but their charm is realized only if the line is smooth. Look at 11 with its *crescendo* and *decrescendo*, one could not bear to hear this sung with a disregard for the composer's markings. In short the singer's line must have firmness, and weight, but it is always soft. This advice is not contradictory.

I draw the singer's attention to his phrase rising from a *pianissimo* to a *piano* (but no more than a *piano*) in 15–16.

Ex. 3

Et — au-tant qu'eulx je de - vien — glo - ri - eux Dès que je pen - se
15   16

There is a *portamento* in the octave fall from the top G sharp which is quite thrilling, especially when it is accomplished gracefully; the tempo is slackened here to give the singer time for this effect. And to the words 'Dès que je pense estre ung peu aymé d'elle' (whene'er I think that perchance she may love me) the piano joins in the singer's tune, an octave below the voice, giving an added sincerity to the words.

The song finishes in the same style that it began, the last faint sound being a repetition of the plucked chord which we enjoyed at the opening (bar 7).

Copyright for the British Empire and permission to reprint by Schott & Co. Ltd.

G   K5338   Mme de Lestang
GSC 22   Maggie Teyte (Gerald Moore)

DER ATLAS

Words by HEINRICH HEINE   *Music by* FRANZ SCHUBERT

ANY singer with a light voice, no matter how much he admires this song or how grand it makes him feel to sing it, is strongly advised to leave it well alone. 'Der Atlas' needs a big voice of such heroic quality and depth that when the singer says 'I am Atlas bearing the weight of the world on my shoulders'—we believe him. (When I say depth of voice I do not necessarily mean that the singer must be a bass nor am I alluding only to the low notes in the stave, for a tenor—the unforgettable Enrico Caruso was an outstanding example—can give us a feeling of depth in his highest notes.)

If ever a song needed an inflexible rhythm from the first note to the last, it is this one, for many of the singer's notes are an octave above the pianoforte's bass and move rhythmically with the latter—as can be seen in Example 1—and it is essential that strict time is observed.

Ex. 1 *Etwas geschwind*

Exact measure is given to the dotted crotchet in bars 5 and 7, to the even notes on 'Atlas' in 6 and 8, to the rest in 6. It can be seen that great precision is necessary to achieve unanimity of attack and to ensure that the strong rhythm is maintained. All the stuffing will be taken out of it if the unwary singer converts the 3/4 into a 9/8 rhythm as follows:

Ex. 2

Compare this flabby affair with the iron muscle of Example 1 and avoid it at all costs.

Schubert gives us the first undotted quaver of the song at bar 15, and this, with the even quavers of 16, must be given the weight that the words demand.

Ex. 3

Weight does not necessarily mean force: bar 16 does not lie in the strongest part of some voices and the amount of tone the singer gives is influenced by the *crescendo* up to 19 where we have a big climax. Weight can be given to 16 by intensifying the diction and by a deliberate spacing of those quavers. The singer will not be overpowered by the pianist here since Schubert thoughtfully inserted a *diminuendo* in the accompaniment at bar 15 to give the performers their chance to make a big *crescendo*. Taking his breath at the quaver rest (17) the singer in one stride climbs that mighty phrase modulating into B minor. I must remind the singer here that his top note at 19 is marked *ff*—not *fff*—he still holds that extra ounce of power in reserve, for it will be needed later.

The middle section, bars 22 to 37, is all suspense; a tenseness that finds no relief or outlet until 39 is reached. This is a testing ground for singer and accompanist, their tone is *piano* but heavy, and their rhythm tightly held.

Ex. 4

The shape of the accompaniment here is entirely different; the roll of thirty-second notes (demisemiquavers) has given way to palpitating triplets whose breathlessness is enhanced by the occasional throb—very pronounced—of the *forte-piano*, as if the unhappy Atlas had almost lost his balance. No pedal is wanted, the sluggardly octaves like heavy foot-falls are detached as marked; they are not *staccato*. Uninfluenced by his partner's triplets, the singer maintains his great rhythm, his semiquavers in 23 and 25 come after the accompanist's chords, not with them. To help the singer to realize an effect of breathlessness in this section, Schubert has cut up the vocal line into short phrases. Only on 'unend-lich' (endless) does he give a long note, and how suggestive this is of a yawning hopeless eternity!

Ex. 5

At 34, 35 we hear in the pianoforte's bass a suggestion that the old rhythm will soon hold sway again. I slur the third beats of 34, 35 feeling that a sliding effect is wanted since they are the only notes in this middle section which are not detached, moreover they

Ex. 6

stamp the spot where the *crescendo* starts its relentless course into the colossal *fff* (38).

This example shows the climbing bass in the pianoforte, but the upward sweep of the voice is far steeper. The singer's even quavers in 37 must stand strongly independent of the triplets beneath him. They must be hammered out.

Bars 39 to the end—similar in pattern to the first section—are howling wind and thunder and the singer has to weather this storm like Ajax defying the lightning. At times the great waves in the accompaniment threaten to engulf him, but no matter, he does his best to rise above them.

49 to 52 has an even greater arch than Example 6 and the singer will, if he can, do the whole phrase in one stride, but if he is forced to breathe—which well may be, remembering that 51 is still *fff*—he should take a quick breath after 'Schmerzen'.

This 'refresher' is readily forgiven for the singer, unlike the accompanist, does not make a *diminuendo* on 'tragen', he keeps up the pressure of tone. His final note anyway is bound to be less in quantity, without him making a conscious diminution. In the accompaniment at 52, the *piano* is only comparative, for the air is still full of rumblings and threats, the octaves in the left hand are still giant strides.

If the pianist has put every ounce of his vitality into this song, if he has thrown into it all his nervous energy (we know the singer expends generously but too often the accompanist is reluctant to give his all either through congenital repression or some mistaken notion of reticence) something will have gone out of him by the time he nears the end. Certainly his right hand will be tiring, nevertheless he must whip up his remaining strength for the last two bars, so that each demisemiquaver of 55 is louder than the last.

The *crescendo* goes on—and this is killing—through the left hand's third beat rest until he lands on the final chord with an almighty crash! It wants some doing.

A most important postscript must be addressed to the accompanist. Do not allow the demisemiquavers in your right hand to lapse into an uncontrolled *tremolo* for this will rob the rhythm of tightness. I have heard 'Der Atlas', 'Die Stadt', 'Die junge Nonne', and many more songs, spoiled by such treatment. Hugo Wolf often asks for it, Schubert hardly ever. Subdivide each beat into four and you will be in no danger of falling into this careless habit and in addition you will be certain that the violent semiquaver after the third beat—which comes so frequently in the first and third sections of this song—will be exact.

Published by Peters

PD 62643	Heinrich Schlusnus (Franz Rupp)
PD 21653	Franz Völker
G ER294	Hans Duhan
PD 62422	Leo Slezak
D LXT2539	Heinrich Schlusnus (Sebastian Peschko)
G P793	Charles Panzéra
D K28314	M. Lichtegg (H. Haeusslein)

DER DOPPELGÄNGER

Words by HEINRICH HEINE   *Music by* FRANZ SCHUBERT

SIX poems by Heinrich Heine are included in the set called Schwanen-gesang (Swan Song). Four of them, 'Ihr Bild', 'Die Stadt', 'Am Meer', 'Der Doppelgänger' (Her Picture, The Town, By the Sea, The Shadow Double) sing of faithless or lost love. The greatest of these wonderful creations is, I think, 'Der Doppelgänger'; its sixty-three bars of music contain a world of woe, they paint a picture which sends an icy chill down your spine. It tells of the lover who, at dead of night, revisits the scene where he once knew happiness, to gaze despairingly at the house where his beloved dwelt long ago. But there in the shadows he is startled to see a ghostly figure waiting as he waits, a man watching as he watches, whose staring eyes, ashen face, and wringing hands seem to mock his own hopeless love. At last, with a heart-rend-ing shudder, the truth dawns on him. The spectre is his very own self.

Confined nearly always to the bass clef, the piano part pays no heed, so far as any change in its *tessitura*, to the three great vocal climaxes. It is stark, but the block harmony surges inexorably forward with slow fixity of purpose which is a sure guide and support for the singer. Be-yond this the latter must fend for himself, since he alone can mould and define his two-bar phrases. Declamatory though the song may be, if the singer conceives the style to be recitative, if he deviates one iota from Schubert's rhythmical design, clips by a hairbreadth a quaver rest, dwells a fraction longer than is asked on one note at the expense of another, then the massive structure of the song will be undermined. The rhythm is tight from the first note to the last except where Schubert says otherwise. And it must be so if inevitability of purpose, from the moment of the story's unfolding until the dénouement, is to be main-tained. For we are witnessing here, not the hysterical raving of imma-ture youth but rather the awful realization of a lifetime wasted. Poem and music may, and indeed should, make our flesh creep but not one bar is without grandeur.

With the playing of the first four chords in the introduction we are arrested, aware of being in the presence of great music. It is here that the unyielding rhythm is established and yet the playing of these chords will not give the accompanist a clue to the basic *tempo*. There is only one way of finding it; the pianist as he plays his introduction must mentally sing the singer's opening phrase 'Still ist die Nacht'. I never play this song without doing so.

139

Ex. 1 *Sehr langsam*

The instruction is *pp* and there is no *crescendo* or *diminuendo*. The chords must be bound together, no daylight between them. To make this perfect joining and to ensure an even distribution of weight on each note of the chord, my fingers are touching the notes in bar 1 before the keys are depressed; as soon as these notes are speaking the sustaining pedal is used to catch the tone. On the third beat of bar 1 my fingers are already touching the notes of the next chord in bar 2. Immediately I hear this chord (but immediately, for there must be no hangover from one chord to another) my right foot releases the pedal and presses it down again to catch the new chord, once again I am enabled to move my fingers well in advance on to the notes of the bar 3 chord. By arranging to touch the notes with time to spare before depressing them, I have more control over touch and weight distribution. No movement of the hands should be obvious to the audience, and the pianist's head and body are perfectly still. This stillness is an aid to the concentration of listeners and performers.

Nearly every phrase of the singer starts on a weak beat of the bar (on the second beat or on a short note just before this beat). He therefore gives full measure to the strong (or first) beat (the crotchet rest, dotted quaver rest, or quaver rest) by stretching it to its fullest value; not by the flicker of an eyelid or an audible intake of breath should he betray any impatience to come in before his time. This should be borne in mind throughout the entire song and especially in the three climaxes (bars 25 to 32, 34 to 41, and 43 to 52). Nothing is easier than to fall into the slovenly and weak-spirited habit of turning the third beat of 5 and the first and third beats of 7 into triplets thus:

Ex. 2

Compared to the Schubertian rhythm how flabby this looks and yet singers are continually doing it.

The antidote is simple, it is to subdivide each beat into four. If when practising, the singer will count twelve semiquavers to a bar, as indicated in Example 3, he will not fail to give each semiquaver its correct value.

Ex. 3

Still ist die Nacht es ru - hen die Gas - sen
5   6   7   8

We all fall occasionally into these careless habits unless we watch ourselves and it is by taking similar measures that singer and pianist will cope clearly with their demisemiquavers in bars 9 and 13, respectively.

Ex. 4

in die - sem Hau - se wohn - te mein Schatz;
9   10   11   12

These quick notes are not grace notes (bar 9) but are full of meaning for they are sung to the word 'this' when the singer says 'in this house dwelt my beloved', and their effect is like a shiver through his body as the eyes of the watcher fix themselves on that house.

In bars 13, 14 the accompaniment echoes the singer's phrase of 11, 12 while the mournful sigh of the quick notes remind us of the singer's shiver (bar 9).

Ex. 5

5 4   3
13   14

These bars and 23–24 (the only time when the right hand forsakes the bass clef) are extremely difficult to play; the prevailing sign is still *pianissimo*, yet the demisemiquavers are intense and need playing with concentration. My fifth, fourth, and third fingers are covering the A natural, G, F sharp a long time before I play them to give me proper control, I am not in so much danger of rushing the quick notes or of arriving on the first beat of 14 with a bump. (In some editions there is a *diminuendo* in 12 as if to warn the player not to rise above *pp*.)

On the second beat of 21 the singer has a turn which I write out in full because I have heard some singers, anxious to improve on Schubert, sing an E sharp instead of E natural. A slow turn is wanted.

Ex. 6

auf dem-sel - ben Platz
21   22

Pianissimo is the rule up to bar 24. It all needs *legato* treatment which the singer should not sacrifice on the altar of dramatic declamation. A *legato* line enhances the eerie atmosphere. The singer of course is living in the song before the pianist plays his first chord, and during all the rests in the vocal line he is singing mentally and holding the audience by his concentration.

We are warned that something startling is about to be told by an accent—still *pianissimo* (like a quick turn of the head)—in the piano part 25 when the singer says 'and there stands a man'. The singer may be in a turmoil of excitement when he hears this accented chord for it marks the beginning of the first of his three great climaxes—each starting low down in the voice, each starting *piano*, each climbing slowly and surely to a *fff* on a top note—yet he maintains control of the rhythm. Yes it is easier to carry each climax to its appointed goal by hurrying, but the singer must resist this temptation. The song should gain in strength. The singer has a long way to go before Schubert wants him to quicken; the terror in the words and music of these ascending passages lies in their inevitability, their inevitability depends on a rigid *tempo*.

Here is a picture of the first climax, 25 to 33:

Ex. 7

How tempting it is for the singer to leap in prematurely at 25, 27, 29, 31—how tempting for the accompanist to hurry too, for he is also subject to human frailty. No, the chord in 24 is given its three full beats

so that the 25 chord does not come too soon; 26, 28, 30 are likewise
justly dealt with. The partners must rehearse this again and again, and
let them experiment by both getting off the track, by hurrying, and
then comparing this effect with a controlled performance. 'Starrt'
(stares) in 27 wants all the time that can be spared—in the *tempo*—
on its two quavers. It is on these two notes, rising a fourth, and by the
intensity that is put into the word, that the listener is gripped by the
throat, warned that something terrific is coming. Every note now
loudens—'und ringt die Hände' (wrings the hands) wants special emphasis on 'ringt' while the chords in the accompaniment have been
growing stronger with each bar culminating in a huge crash on 31 before the singer's 'vor Schmerzensgewalt' (agony of sorrow). 32 is slightly
less than 31, and this is important for were it otherwise the vocal line,
now dropping an octave, would be swamped by the pianoforte tone.
Also by dropping his tone slightly at 32 the accompanist has more
chance to execute his sharp *diminuendo* which follows. This *diminuendo*
from a *fortissimo* to a *piano* in two bars happened very easily on Schubert's own piano, the tone just naturally went to nothing. Not so the
modern pianoforte. The latter, it is true, cannot sustain like a voice or
a string. As soon as a note is struck it starts to decrease in quantity; but
such a proposition as the steep *diminuendo* in 32 and 33 would be beyond
it unless aided by the player. Something must be done to help. As soon
as I hear this *ff* chord I put down the soft pedal and hold it right
through the *diminuendo*. But that is not enough. Immediately I have
struck the chord, down goes my sustaining pedal, then still holding this
sustaining pedal I raise my fingers from the keys and at once press them
gently down again without sounding them. The keys being depressed
again with the fingers, I take off the sustaining pedal—press it down
again—release and catch the notes again with the fingers and so on.
This operation can be done several times during the course of these two
bars, and of course at 41, 42 and 52, 53. It may sound complicated and
my explanation involved but how simple it is to perform can be seen
from the following diagram; moreover it is invisible to the audience.

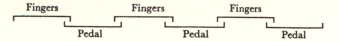

As I say, the effect of this will be a much steeper *diminuendo*, averting
a *subito piano* on 34.

The building up of the second climax starts from 34 and still the
tempo is held back unyieldingly. 'Mir graust es' (I shudder) is of verbal
rather than tonal significance, the *crescendo* should not be anticipated
as the singer saves up, if possible, for an even bigger *crescendo* than before,
on to

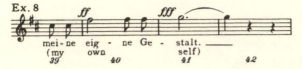

No *diminuendo* on 'Gestalt', the final 't' in the word is hit violently, giving realism to the frightful disclosure.

Now comes the longest of these climbing passages and at last Schubert asks for an *accelerando*. The effect of this *accelerando* is terrific; but not if we have made it previously. It is started immediately after the chord in 43—is maintained through 'du bleicher Geselle' (you pallid companion) and through 'was äffst du nach mein Liebesleid' (why do you mock my grief). 'Äffst' (mock) will stand as much venom as the singer can put into it. Until now the pianoforte began the climbing sections with the same figure as it started the song (1 to 4) but here it ascends chromatically to the bitter chord on the word 'äffst'.

This *accelerando* is felt until the first F sharp in 49 (second syllable of 'gequält')

but the last three quavers in this bar should be drawn out so that 'Stelle' is not hurried at all.

At 51 the old *tempo* reigns again, thus the agony of the climax 'so manche Nacht' (so many a night) is not short-lived.

Ex. 11

So much energy and breath will have been expended on the F sharp that the word 'Nacht' is bound to be less in tone, but none the less it will still be big. Care has to be taken, therefore, that the following word 'in' (after a breath) has the same volume as 'Nacht'. Two pitfalls await the unwary on this 'in'. The first is that with the new breath the singer is prone to attack with too much vigour—for it is a falling phrase from 52 to the end; and the other, exactly the reverse, is for the singer to begin his 'in' too softly, leaving no room for the gradual softening which runs through 54, 55, 56. This ability to reduce tonal volume to practically nothing must be imitated by the pianist, who will want an even softer chord at 62 than at 60.

Ex. 12

Looking at the song as a whole, singer and pianist would be wise to treat the first twenty bars with profundity certainly, but—in view of all that is to follow—with some reticence. 'Meine eigne Gestalt' and 'so manche Nacht' are the two great pinnacles of the song, yet neither must dwarf the other. They both demand tremendous tone and all the singer's power yet they are different in character; the first is all horror while the second is the fearful collapse of all resistance: at 'so manche Nacht' the heart breaks. The tear-choked retrospect with which Aksel Schiøtz and Herbert Janssen sing 'in alter Zeit' is infinitely moving.

We should be sensitive of Schubert's genius which can transfigure by magic such a phrase as 'sie hat schon längst die Stadt verlassen' (she has left the town long ago). Those bars 15, 16 are parallel to 5, 6 and many a composer would have been content to treat both phrases alike,

in which case we should have had

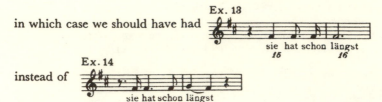

Ex. 13

sie hat schon längst
15   *16*

instead of

Ex. 14

sie hat schon längst

What a world of sorrow on the word 'längst'. And again the implication of permanence by the slow turn on 21: the modulation on 59 from the D major to the C major chord (a chord which sends a sharp pang through one's body)

Ex. 15

These and other inflexions the student can discover to his unending wonder.

'Der Doppelgänger' takes nearly five minutes to perform.

Published by Peters

C	L2135	Alexander Kipnis (Frank Bibb)
PD	62643	Heinrich Schlusnus
P	R020217	Richard Tauber
G	DB1184	Feodor Chaliapin
PD	95102	Heinrich Rehkemper
O	25446	P. Lohmann
G	DB1833	Therese Schnabel (Artur Schnabel)
G	ES507	Hans Duhan
G	DB5797	Herbert Janssen (Gerald Moore)
C	LX1004	Hans Hotter (Herman von Nordberg)
G	DB4948	Charles Panzéra
C	71509D	Lotte Lehmann (Paul Ulanowsky)
G	DB5523	Gerhard Hüsch
G	DB10087	Marko Rothmüller (S. Gyr)
D	LXT2543	Gérard Souzay (Jacqueline Bonneau)
P	E10758	Franz Steiner (Michael Raucheisen)
P	R30046	Nicola Rossi-Lemeni (G. Favaretto)
D	K2109	Paul Schoeffler (Ernest Lush)
V	12-0580	Marian Anderson (Franz Rupp)
C	DCX47	Ivar Andresen
PD	66434	Fritz Soot
D	K28315	M. Lichtegg (H. Haeusslein)

ERLKÖNIG

Poem by GOETHE

Music by FRANZ SCHUBERT
Op. 1

so often, after hearing a performance of this song, the only impression left in the mind of the listener is of its relentless speed. Energetic galloping, however, is not the be-all and end-all of the song. Of course it does fly forward inexorably and the two performers strain every nerve, give their last ounce of strength to maintain this urge. Spend their energy, drive themselves forward as they may, the performers should always bear in mind that, above all considerations of speed, it is the drama of the story that matters. Most of this drama is in the singer's part, and the accompanist should always bear this in mind in spite of the fact that the galloping horse, which first catches the eye in this picture and clatters throughout the song, is drawn in the terrific accompaniment.

It is the singer who makes the wind whistle through our hair. He makes us share the terror of the dying boy, the anguish of the father; it is he who lets us hear the spectral Erlking's grim overtures grow from a sinister smile to a scowl, from a whisper to a snarl.

Each of these widely distinct characters must be delineated according to his own nature, invested with his individuality. There is a world of difference between all three. When he is the boy, the singer should be petrified with fear down to the very marrow of his bones; when he is the father he is at once the comforting protector of his child and a prey to the most tormenting anxiety; when he is the Erlking he is Death, implacable, ghastly.

To people the stage with this assorted caste the singer shares their emotions and conveys these emotions to us, and the picture becomes alive. But we are not gripped nor is our pulse quickened if the singer thinks he can carry us away by merely wearing a different facial expression for each character. Schubert, however, comes to our aid, and it is very necessary for the singer to be intelligently aware of his masterly design. He sets the vocal line of the father on a different level to that of the boy. See, in the following example, how the *tessitura* of the child's voice lies compared to the man's.

Ex.1

147

This difference between these two voices is always quite distinct. True, the vocal line 37 to 40 is an ascending one, but it is naturally so, for a troubled question is being posed, 'My son, why do you cover your face in fear?' At 51 to 54, low again in the voice, the father attempts to comfort the boy and make light of his fears: we can tell it by the *tessitura* as well as by the words. A still further distinction between these voices is to be seen in Schubert's instructions. Nearly always the father speaks in a normal tone of voice—often it is marked *piano* (note for instance the *diminuendo* at 80, Example 2) to prevent his increasing agitation from alarming the boy further. The latter loses control of himself certainly—but the father never, he dare not. True the vocal line of the father gets higher and higher as his worry increases—we can see it by comparing Examples 1, 2, and 3—but it is always far below the level of the boy's in pitch and in fever.

Ex. 2

The further the song progresses the more shrill, the more frenzied the child becomes,

Ex. 3

until at last demented, he screams

Ex.4

fff CHILD

Mein Va - ter, mein Va - ter, jetzt · fasst er mich an!
124   *125*   *126*   *127*

Erl - kö - nig hat mir ein Leids ge - tan!
128   *129*   *130*   *131*

We can see by the quavers in 74, 99, 125 the trembling child cowering closer to his father's breast.

To sum up, then, as far as we have gone: each wail of the child 'mein Vater, mein Vater' is louder and shriller than the last. Schubert has made it possible to achieve this vocal effect by stepping up the line at each succeeding entry of the boy; he has made it possible to get into the character of the father by keeping that vocal line low in pitch and quantity. I do not think that Schubert is asking too much of the singer.

One character is sung with restraint, with deep manly timbre of voice, and a facial expression of lively but controlled anxiety.

The other character is sung without restraint other than that which tells the singer that he must have vocal force in hand for the huge build-up to the climax.

The dreaded Erlking I have left until last because I feel that Schubert has depicted him so marvellously that he presents less difficulty so far as vocal characterization is concerned, than the other characters. The singer's voice for the Erlking must be disembodied, it never rises above a *pianissimo* level; only the child hears him. He sings with a leer, a malignant smile. Were it not for this smile the part could be sung with almost clenched teeth. The tempter paints a picture of pretty games and flowers, of nightly revels with his daughters, a picture he tries to make alluring but which, because of this ghastly smile, repels the boy. Almost a nasal tone is required for his three utterances, a reedy tone which the singer can get by taking full advantage of the numerous thin vowel sounds met so frequently when the Erlking sings; I put them in the following example in italics.

Ex.5

pp ERLKÖNIG

Du *lie* - bes *Kind*, komm, *geh*   *mit*   *mir!*   gar
        58   *59*   *60*   *61*

schö - ne *Spie* - le *spiel*   *ich* *mit* *dir*;   *etc.*
        62   *63*   *64*   *65*

These thin vowel sounds are employed again and again by the Erlking, in his second invitation

> 'Willst, feiner Knabe, du mit mir gehn?
> Meine Töchter sollen dich warten schön;
> Meine Töchter führen den nächtlichen Reihn
> Und wiegen und tanzen und singen dich ein.'

I can count at least sixteen vowels that can be made thin and mean; if the singer can find more so much the better. Listening to Fischer-Dieskau or Hans Hotter singing this section, one is convinced that this was Goethe's intention, for these artists give the Erlking's speeches softly but thrill the listener by the pointedness of their enunciation. Schubert marks this section *ppp*.

Only once the Erlking emerges from his *sotto voce*; this occurs on his last word to the boy 'und bist du nicht willig, so brauch ich Gewalt'. (And if you're unwilling I'll seize you by force.) 'Gewalt' stands out suddenly in sharp relief, like a snarl: Schubert marks this word *fff* as the cruel icy hand clutches its victim.

I have accounted for six of the eight verses of the poem, that is to say verses 2 to 7 inclusive. The first and last verses are narrative. Verse 1 describes the scene—the rider galloping through the night with his dying child clasped to his breast: the last verse tells of the father's shudder, of the spurring of his horse to greater speed, and the arrival home to find the child dead in his arms. The horse is pulled up to a standstill (I do not think a *rallentando* in 145, before coming to a halt in the following bar, is out of order even though Schubert does not mark it, for the sweating steaming animal could not be brought from a furious gallop to a full stop in one stride) and with a passage in recitative style the song finishes.

Ex.6

The pianist gets his diminished seventh chord in 147 out of the way before the singer says 'war tot' (was dead). This must be sung *piano* as the composer marks; it is more impressive than a *forte* after the screaming and tumult that preceded it. Strict observance of the *fermata* rest is necessary, and a slight but significant break before the final word 'tot'.

Now for the accompaniment.

Many an honest pianist finding this accompaniment impossible to play is in good company, for Schubert himself jumped up from the piano in a rage exclaiming, "The triplets are too difficult for me"; but I submit with all respect that it was much easier to play them on the instrument of Schubert's day with its light butterfly touch than it is on a modern concert grand pianoforte.

Some singers take no heed of the *tempo* established in the introduction and run away at virtually an impossible speed. What is the just *tempo*? Schubert marked it 'Schnell' (quick) and that is clear enough, but the rhythm of the repeated octaves and chords represents the rapid *staccato* of thudding hooves. Imagine for a moment the triplet rhythm of a galloping horse; you will find if you are really fair that it is possible to mutter 'cloppitty, cloppitty, cloppitty' ever so much faster than a horse could possibly gallop.

Singers should bear this in mind as it is their responsibility, for certainly no pianist is going to establish a *tempo* that is ridiculously and unreasonably fast. And besides, at 135, when his right hand is already at collapsing point, the accompanist is asked to go even faster. No, I think the clue to the true *tempo* is to be found in the left-hand motif.

Ex. 7

Of course the song is fast; there is no gainsaying that, but this figure must intimidate us and it cannot do that if it is scrambled. It is robbed of its meaning if taken too rapidly.

I alluded above to the 'honest' accompanist. It is practically certain that he will be unable to play the repeated right-hand octaves and chords as they are written: therefore he must be dishonest, and take care not to advertise his delinquency. For instance, when the left hand is doing nothing it is unreasonable to make the right hand do all the work and expect it to be able to maintain its speed and strength for very long.

Ex. 8 *Schnell*

Obviously the left hand can help by taking the lower note. Here are bars 1 to 3 enough to give the reader the idea. I do not improve on Schubert by altering his notes, I only rearrange them, showing my fingering.

So far so good, but 6 and 7 become complicated by an added note in the right hand which we cope with as follows:

Again at 15, 16, &c., the left hand helps and comes over above the right hand, and springs out of the way.

I think the above examples suffice to show the pianist how he can save his right hand whenever there is a rest or a pedal note in the bass clef.

In spite of all his manœuvring, however, the most willing horse will be hard put to it at the child's final outburst at 123. Here it may be necessary to resort to subterfuge:

But if he performs this makeshift arrangement boldly by playing his left-hand quavers forcibly, it may escape detection; that, as I said earlier, is the principal consideration. What a respite for the right hand is provided by those quaver rests!

Such means as I have suggested for negotiating these problems of technique and endurance are surely forgivable in view of what comes at 131 and for which I can offer no relief.

Ex. 13

There are fifteen bars of this; it is killing and too much for the strength of any man. A generous use of the sustaining pedal will help.

Two periods of rest for the accompanist are bars 58 to 71 and bars 87 to 96. I give the first two bars of each of these sections. They occur when the Erlking is whispering to the boy.

Ex. 14

Ex. 15

In Examples 14 and 15, the latter especially, the pianist rests his hand by allowing it to go limp and relaxed. He will feel refreshed when he has to renew his vigorous clatter later. Neither of these sections are at all fatiguing to play, for the pianoforte tone needs only to correspond with the singer's whisper.

I once had the pleasure (the doubtful pleasure) of hearing a virtuoso pianist play the Erlking. It was, from the technical standpoint, an astounding and unbelievably brilliant performance. It had but one impediment; the singer—young, strong, hard working though he was- - was unable to make himself heard above the general din that his famous partner was creating. It is worthy of the pianist's notice that out of the song's 148 bars, 69 of them are *piano* or *pianissimo*. This great song is the severest test imaginable for the two performers. All I have attempted is to indicate how a singer can bring the picture with all its drama to life. The accompanist who is forced to dodge some of the technical difficulties in the manner I have sketched can remain unashamed so long as his conscience tells him he is endeavouring to do his best by Schubert. I can only hope the reader of goodwill assumes it is unnecessary for me to adopt these measures.

Although 'Erlkönig' is a man's song, I have heard wonderful performances by two great women artists, Elena Gerhardt and Kathleen Ferrier.

Published by Peters

Voc	A0215	Elena Gerhardt (Ivor Newton)
PD	67051	Heinrich Schlusnus
G	DB1484	Sigrid Onegin
V	7177	Ernestine Schumann-Heink (Katherine Hoffman)
C	30019	David Bispham
G	ES508	Hans Duhan
G	DB1836	Therese Schnabel (Artur Schnabel)
PD	19857	Lula Mysz-Gmeiner
O	6818	Michael Bohnen
C	9431	Frank Titterton
C	C1327	Peter Dawson (Gerald Moore)
C	L2038	Norman Allin
C	9088	Muriel Brunskill
C	DB4948	Charles Panzéra
C	LX665	Alexander Kipnis (Gerald Moore)
C	DB21350	Dietrich Fischer-Dieskau (Gerald Moore)
G	DB5625	Frida Leider (Michael Raucheisen)
G	DB5523	Gerhard Hüsch
G	DB10088	Marko Rothmüller (S. Gyr)
O	80004	Lilli Lehman
V	6122	Johanna Gadski (Frank la Forge)
PD	66006	Heinrich Rehkemper
G	C3925	Bernard Sönnerstedt (Gerald Moore)
D	LXT2543	Gérard Souzay (Jacqueline Bonnèau)
G	DB6010	Alexander Kipnis (C. Dougherty)
G	DB3361	Marta Fuchs (Michael Raucheisen)
V	10-1448	Lotte Lehmann (Paul Ulanowsky)
G	D1276	Robert Radford
G	DB1148	Maria Jeritza
V	6273	Ernestine Schumann-Heink

DIE FORELLE

Words by SCHUBART   *Music by* FRANZ SCHUBERT
Op. 32

STANDING on the edge of a stream, the singer sees in its clear depths a trout darting joyously. An angler is doing his best to catch the trout, and the song describes the duel between the two. Our hero is the fish, while the angler is the villain of the piece. As long as the angler plays the game he gains no advantage over the fish but when he muddies the stream by stirring up the water his victim is caught. This method of cheating the trout by no means meets with the onlooker's approval— it is not cricket. He refers in the most scathing terms to the fisherman.

Anyone who has appreciated the sinuous movement of a fish as it shoots along with two or three flicks of its tail—then gently glides, flicks and glides again, can see how Schubert has suggested this in the accompaniment. Almost throughout the entire song the rhythmical pattern remains the same with the flickering semiquaver figure in the first half of the bar and the moveless glide in the second half. To convey this picture a slight *rubato* should be allowed. (Too slavish an adherence to the metronome, an insistence on a robot-like rhythm becomes monotonous. When uniformity comes in by one door interest goes out by the other.) I feel that the second half of the bar may occasionally, but not with regularity, be given a fraction more time than the first half of the bar by the slightest *tenuto* on the accented quaver. I am almost afraid of suggesting this *rubato* in case it should be exaggerated. Let me put it this way. If, for argument's sake, a bar lasts two seconds, the second half of the bar might take a tenth of a second longer than the first half. Naturally it is as undesirable as it is impossible to measure in this way, but it gives an idea how infinitesimal this departure from regularity should be. Let us see for the moment how the foregoing applies to the pianoforte introduction; we shall note later how the words call for it from time to time.

Ex. 1   *Etwas lebhaft*

155

The comparison I made above to the movement of a fish can be carried even further. We can say that in bar 1 he is near the surface of the stream, in 2 and 3 deeper, in 4 and 5 at the river bottom and almost indiscernible. A careful perusal of Schubert's markings will prove that the composer must have had some such message to impart to us by the descent through three octaves of the flickering figure and by the reduction in tone from a *piano* to a *pianissimo*. Does the reader accuse me of exaggerating Schubert's intentions out of all proportion? Well, better that than sticking in the mud at the bottom of the stream with one's imagination bogged down.

The semiquavers are even, in time and tone—with no *crescendo* up to the accented note. A liquid touch is wanted without semblance of jerk or angularity. Above all, no accent must be made on the fourth quaver of each bar. I attach great importance to the transparent playing of this introduction since the singer's first words are 'In einem Bächlein helle' (In a streamlet clear)—the texture must not be obscure in any way; therefore no sustaining pedal is wanted except for a momentary touch on the last quaver of bar 3 to enable the hands to take their leap with smoothness—and later to hold the chord in bar 6.

Quite frequently the singer will want to take a thought more time over this second half of a bar. In verse 1, for example, he might like to do it at 15 and 17.

Ex. 2

Ich stand an dem Ge - sta - de und sah in sü - sser Ruh

The first syllable of 'süsser' askes for it plainly because of the meaning of the words, and 15 suggests it through the graceful semiquaver figuration.

In studying this type of song, which is as near to *strophic* as makes no matter, the performers should look for an opportunity to make a slight variation in rhythm or dynamics in order to bring more life and sparkle to their performance. Thus 21, 45, 71 are in strict time, while 25, 49, 75, have slight stresses on the two final quavers.

Ex. 3

Bars 21, 46, 71   Bars 25, 49, 75

Not only is this more refreshing than repeating the phrase again and
again in the same way, but it is more friendly and prepares the way for
the accompanist's *rubato* treatment of his little interlude which always
follows. Schubert would not have objected to this rhythmic freedom
provided it were not overdone. How delicately he himself varies the
four quavers of 19 into decorative semiquavers at 23.

Ex. 4

Bars 19, 43, 69   Bars 23, 47, 73

Words as well as music must be brought to life, and the singer
anxious to give point to his story will see word stresses which it is
impossible for a composer to indicate. For instance 'so lang dem
Wasser Helle,— (so dacht ich,)— nicht gebricht' (as long as the water
remains clear, thought I, no need to worry) is all so much clearer to the
listener if the singer makes a slight break without breathing before and
after the parenthetical 'so dacht ich'. Again 'launische' (cunning), 11;
'Fischer' (angler), 31; 'nicht' (not), 50; 'Zuckte' (quivered), 64—all of
which come on the first beat—can be underlined. This emphasis does
not necessitate a sudden increase in tone but a sharpening of the
enunciation.

However it is most undesirable for the song to be sung in a winsome,
arch, or coy manner. Neither should it be 'acted'. I remember one
singer who gave the audience a glassy gaze when she sang 'sah's mit
kaltem Blute' (observes unfeelingly), who became as frosty as a step-
mother at the word 'Diebe' (thief) and was a tragedy queen when the
little fish expired. A mountain out of a molehill.

The comfortable semiquaver ripple in the accompaniment is
interrupted at 55

Ex. 5

Doch end - lich ward dem Die - be

55   56

by a more agitated figure reflecting the singer's indignation, while the stirring up of the stream—the *legato* line being omitted for the first time—can be seen at 59 to 61. Energy is needed to play the dark muddy chords in the bass, always remembering that a purling stream is being disturbed by a stick, not an ocean lashed by a typhoon—a trout is about to be landed, not a whale. I like an increased speed here to portray the apprehension of the sympathetic onlooker and the agitation, or at the very least, concern of the fish. All through this section the rhythm must be tight, with no *rubato*. A preparatory easing of the *tempo* at 67 will bring us back to the old *tempo* at 68 whence the song resumes the even tenor of its way, the onlooker consoling himself apparently with the philosophical reflection that there are as many good fish in the sea as ever came out of it.

Altogether it is a light-hearted affair and should be sung with the smiling humour of an Irmgard Seefried.

Published by Peters

O	6567	Lotte Schöne
G	DA835	Elena Gerhardt (Paula Hegner)
G	DA4856	Charles Panzéra
PD	21456	Lula Mysz-Gmeiner
G	DA989	Vanni-Marcoux
G	P847	Willy Tubiana
G	DA1586	Kirsten Flagstad (Edwin MacArthur)
G	DA1550	Marian Anderson (K. Vehanen)

C	DB837	Dorothy Stanton (Gerald Moore)
C	LB77	Elisabeth Schwarzkopf (Karl Hudez)
PD	62551	Fritz Soot
G	DA1852	Elisabeth Schumann (Gerald Moore)
C	DB2999	Isobel Baillie (Gerald Moore)
T	A10426	Erna Sack (William Czernik)
G	DA6010	Ria Ginster (Paul Baumgartner)
D	M658	Suzanne Danco (G. Agosti)
V	87104	Ernestine Schumann-Heink
G	62855	Heinrich Schlusnus (Sebastian Peschko)
G	DB2481	Ria Ginster (Gerald Moore)

MEERES STILLE

Words by GOETHE   *Music by* FRANZ SCHUBERT
                                                      Op. 3 No. 2

DEEP silence reigns over the waters. The sea seems asleep, yet the
becalmed boatman views with anxious eyes its ominous smoothness.
Not a breath of air is felt in the threatening death-like stillness, not a
wave disturbs the ocean.

Schubert, in depicting here the calm before the storm, gives us one
of his most impressive pictures. For the singer, it is a severe test, the
long phrases must be delivered unwaveringly, with an almost oily
smoothness. The sea is moveless, there is no rise and fall, so the singer
makes no nuances but keeps to *pianissimo* always. When Elena Gerhardt
sang 'Keine Luft von keiner Seite' her tone was almost disembodied,
there was literally not a breath of air to be felt. Hans Hotter subdued
his big voice to a whisper so that you were conscious of the strength
of the sea even though it was sleeping. 'Tiefe Stille herrscht im Wasser'
needs a big voice used with infinite quietness. But what a problem it is
for the singer!

The most experienced artists approach this song with trepidation,
so slowly does it move and so long are the phrases. Nor does the
accompaniment appear to help. The voice seems naked and exposed
above the bare broken chords of the piano part.

Ex. 1

These four bars take between twelve and fifteen seconds to sing.

It is interesting, I think, to note that in heart-rending songs such
as 'Doppelgänger' or 'Ihr Bild', Schubert contents himself with the
simple instruction 'Sehr Langsam' or 'Langsam': before the great
'Erlkönig' he merely writes 'Schnell', while 'etwas Geschwind' suffices
for the terrifying 'Gruppe aus dem Tartarus'. Here, however, in
'Meeres Stille' Schubert almost spreads himself by adding the word
'ängstlich'—anxiously. In those first four bars the singer by his serious

demeanour, by his controlled colourlessness of tone makes us aware that the deep stillness of the sleeping waters is not the calm of a cloudless smiling day; the skies are grey, the sea is sullen.

It is imperative, in my opinion, that the top note of the pianoforte chord synchronizes with the singer's note. Written out in full, therefore, the first two bars would be

Ex . 2

It would be quite wrong, I feel, to do it like this.

Ex. 3

I said earlier that the accompaniment does not appear to help. The operative word is 'appear'. For a great responsibility is thrown on the accompanist—he can help the singer in no uncertain way to find the time to breathe unhurriedly and steadily so that the long vocal line can be sustained. Working on this song with Flora Nielsen, one of our finest singers, I discovered that some of the *arpeggiando* chords are slower than the others. That is to say they can be made slower when the singer needs a breath. A breath will be needed at least every fourth bar throughout the song, after bars 4, 8, 12, 16, 20, 24, 28 and it is while these breaths are taken that the accompanist makes his *arpeggiandi* more slowly.

The Example 4 shows the generous time allowance the singer can take for her breath. These big breaths are only taken at the seven bars I mentioned earlier (4, 8, 12, 16, 20, 24, 28), any other breaths required must be snatched as they may.

Seeing those wide gaps in 4 and 8 an objection might be made (but not by singers) that we are making three beats to those bars instead of two. It is only too true. But to mitigate this offence to some slight extent I would suggest that these breaths do not need so much time allowance at the beginning of the song as they do in the second half, when the singer will be hard pressed to keep the voice soft, steady, and sustained. The intelligent co-operative listener will be so absorbed by the mood Schubert's genius evokes that he will be grateful to any singer who gives it to him without disturbing the brooding calm.

Published by Peters

OL	30	Erika Rokyta (Noel Gallon)
C	LX1305	Hans Hotter (Gerald Moore)
ALLO	AL27	R. Herbert (F. Waldman)

DER TOD UND DAS MÄDCHEN

Poems by CLAUDIUS

Music by FRANZ SCHUBERT
Op. 7 No. 3

THE maiden tosses feverishly on her bed of sickness, she is terrified at the approach of Death. 'Go away, you grisly skeleton,' she gasps, 'I am too young to die.'

Death's shadowy figure is seen in the pianoforte introduction, therefore the *alla breve* sign must not give a false impression of speed; the accompanist adopts the same tempo that the singer will want at 'Gib deine Hand', bar 22. *Legato* playing is needed, unaffected but intense, with the weight evenly distributed on each note so that the inner parts are not lost. It is all mysterious.

During the playing of this eight-bar introduction which takes nearly half a minute, the singer assumes the frame of mind of the maiden. Like her he becomes aware of the presence of Death; he breathes in ever-quickening gasps until—in the short silence before the vocal entry at 8—his face expresses terror. Naturally this quickened breathing is physically disturbing to the singer, but this is preferable to the ease or complacency that a finely controlled tone would suggest. Schubert has marked this breathless section 'Somewhat faster', and it is at least half as fast again as the opening speed of the introduction: this new *tempo* comes without warning and if the performers are decisive about it, its suddenness startles the listener.

Ex. 1 *Etwas geschwinder*
(DAS MÄDCHEN)

Vor - ü - ber ach, vor - ü - ber! geh, wil - der Knochenmann! Ich

bin noch jung geh, Lie - ber! und rüh - re mich nicht

Look at the short utterances of 9 to 15; there are no less than five breaths, including one after 'Knochenmann'. Although the *crescendo* is marked on bar 12 it is quite natural to anticipate it, for the whole section climbs feverishly from the first note up to 13 and 14, the height of the fever, and from thence it gradually abates; yet this *crescendo* should only suggest more and more agitation. It does not call for a great increase of tone—and 'jung' is more important than 'bin', despite the latter's high note.

But the paroxysm fades. With it, resistance and strength fade too, it is with entreaty rather than execration that the words 'Let me be' are uttered. At bar 16 the accompaniment shows us that Death has taken charge. He has placed his cool hand on the burning brow: the vocal line descends to the lowest note in the girl's voice. The accent on bar 17 is indicative of a sigh. Already the terror has left her at 18 (and left the singer) as she comes under the soothing spell of the Comforter. Her last words are uttered without resistance.

During the slight *rallentando* of 20 and 21, and during the *fermata* of utter silence—which should be prolonged rather than abbreviated—the singer assumes a different character, he has ample time here in which to compose himself after the fluttering breath of the opening phrases. His physiognomy which in turn mirrored terror, entreaty, and resignation, now assumes an expression of majestic serenity, for a different voice—Death—is about to speak; a voice calm and deep, a voice which, though employed in the softest and tenderest fashion, is suggestive of limitless power, not the puny whisper of a mortal. The *pianissimo* tone must be resonant and well supported. Resuming the slow *tempo* of the piano introduction, Death says

Ex. 2 *Das erste Zeitmass*

There are sixteen D's whose hypnotic reiteration is relieved of any threat of monotony by the gentle smoothing out of 'strafen' (punish), 28, 29. Without increase of tone, emphasis can be given to the word 'Freund' by allowing the 'F' and rolling 'R' of the word to take their time. It wants a little generosity of feeling—a feeling that will be easily awakened by the consciousness of the upward-moving bass in 26, 27, 28.

Death's anxiety to comfort in 30 to 33 is shown by his almost eager insistence on a higher note for his repeated monotone—this time the 'F'. He raises his voice slightly at this point before softening the tone from 34 to the end.

'Sollst sanft' are tender words, and for the sake of their meaning should be given distinctly and unhurriedly.

It has been held that Death in this song is a sinister malevolent figure. Chaliapin used the song as a vehicle for his great tragical gifts, his visage was grim with foreboding, his giant figure threatening when he sang to the maiden. Hearing this performance one succumbed to the spell of it and was made to shudder by the strength of this artist's character acting. To many musicians the Chaliapin idea is so entirely convincing that they will hear of no alternative. Their rejoinder to the suggestion that Death's words are comforting in the extreme, pain-assuaging to body and mind, is that Death is a horrible spectre, his words a mockery and a delusion.

Yet I can see no justification for this conception of the song.

The composer of 'The Erlking' knew how to frighten us when he wished. 'Erlkönig' is sheer terror from beginning to end—'und bist du nicht willig, so brauch ich Gewalt' (if you are not willing I'll seize you by force); so is 'Gruppe aus dem Tartarus' with its 'Hohl sind ihre Augen', &c.; so are 'Der Zwerg' and 'Der Doppelgänger'. All these are well-known examples of Schubert's power to make our flesh creep whenever the occasion demanded. That he did not conceive this to be such an occasion is proved, in my opinion, by the slow majestic chorale from bar 22 to the end, all of which is balm after the frenzy, painted with so sure a hand, of bars 9 to 15.

Where is the deceit in the moving and simple 'bin Freund und komme nicht zu strafen' with the word 'Nicht' harmonically stressed and 'strafen' placed in the soothing major key? Where the malice in 'ich bin nicht wild' with those easeful chords in the accompaniment? And the left hand's descending bass notes to 'sollst sanft', are these not heavenly rather than devilish, as Schubert finally brings us, as if with a benediction, into the serene haven of D major 'in meinen Armen schlafen'?

The words and the music tell us that the approach of Death at first struck the maiden with horror, but they also tell us with equal certainty that Death is no Avenging Angel, that he lulls the maiden's fears, eases her suffering and gathers her, softly and safely to his arms.

Singers frequently take the lower octave on the second syllable of 'schlafen' (37), indeed Richard Capell, whose book *Schubert Songs* (Benn) should be within reach of every student and lover of Schubert, lays it down that it wants a low D. Without wishing to cross swords with so great an authority, I must confess to a personal preference for a return to the same D with which this section begins: the lower octave disturbs me since he who attempts it, unless the singer be a Kipnis, a Mack Harrell or a Norman Allin, is often forced to accentuate it in the effort to get deep down into the centre of the note. Whichever of the two notes is chosen, however, let it be remembered that this second syllable is less in volume than the first. The absolute peace which 'schlafen' needs is helped by the minutest predominance of the pianoforte F sharps in bars 36, 37.

Published by Peters

P	R020061	Lotte Lehmann
G	E589	Maria Olszewska
P	E10744	Karin Branzell
PD	21457	Lula Mysz-Gmeiner
G	DA607	Ernestine Schumann-Heink
C	5019	Norman Allin
G	DB1184	Feodor Chaliapin
V	10-1327	Marian Anderson (Franz Rupp)
T	E1687	Aullikki Rautawaara (Franz Rupp)
G	DA1550	Marian Anderson (Kosti Vehanen)

C   1382   Ernestine Schumann-Heink
G   DA6022   E. Fink (S. Gyr)
Cla MD9601   Margarete Klose (H. Wetzel)
G   EJ41   Julia Culp
O   188734   Ninon Vallin
O   25561   P. Lohmann

DER NUSSBAUM

Words by MOSEN   *Music by* ROBERT SCHUMANN
                                                    Op. 25

THE leaves and blossom of an almond tree, softly rustling in the night breeze by the window of a sleeping maiden, are whispering to her. The maiden, loving and longing, cannot understand what they are saying until finally after continual repetition the meaning of the message becomes clear to her and she smiles in her dreams.

This little enigma is posed in the accompaniment and runs all through the song:

It happens a score of times in different guises, but it tries most insistently to make itself understood when it appears thus, in the tonic key. The answer to this riddle is not supplied until near the end, when we are told 'The leaves whisper of a bridegroom next year.' But the significance of this phrase lies in the fact that for the first and only time throughout the song, the singer sings the above figure in the same key in which the accompanist has been playing it so often; a subtle and charming way of letting us know that the message has been heard and understood.

It has all been beautifully and delicately conceived by the composer, but it is necessary that the singer and pianist should realize the import of this constantly recurring theme; being in the secret, knowing the solution, their singing and playing become tender and informed.

Every phrase of the singer and its echo in the accompaniment is shaped like the branch of a tree—it rises and then falls a little, and like the branch tapers off towards the tip. That is to say we *crescendo* on the rising curve and *diminuendo* on the downward curve. This treatment gives verisimilitude and shapeliness to the vocal phrase but in addition it enables the singer to avoid a jarring clash with the pianist on bar 5.

Ex. 3

Es grü - net ein Nuss - baum vor dem Haus,

There is an ugly dissonance if 'Haus' is held while bar 5 is being played. Two methods of avoiding this—both of which are obnoxious to me—are very frequently used. The first is for the accompanist to hold up proceedings and not start bar 5 until the singer has seen fit to relinquish her 'Haus': this of course causes an unshapely disturbance to the music's rhythmical sway. The other method is for the singer to clip her note abruptly at the end of the bar like snapping off a twig. But surely the branches should be allowed to sway gently and uninterruptedly, and this the singer allows if the word 'Haus' is tapered off. Her consonant at the end of the word can come on the first beat of 5 so long as we do not hear her vowel in this bar: thus too the flowing rhythm is preserved. The opening six bars of 'Nussbaum' should be rehearsed again and again for the situation I have been describing arises at 14–15, 24–25, 44–45, 48–49 and at 40.

Vocal and piano parts are performed with the greatest possible smoothness and softness but not at the expense of movement; taken too slowly the music loses the swaying motion that is so essential to the picture ('neigend, beugend zierlich zum Kusse die Häuptchen zart'). Especially at 9 and 29 the singer takes care that her voice does not swell disproportionately on her high F sharp;

Ex. 4

er blätt - rig die Blät - ter aus.
zum Kus - se die Häupt - chen zart.
9 and 29

she should bear in mind that the word 'flüstern' (whispers) comes five times, so that never during the song does the tone need more than a *mezzopiano*.

Occasionally Schumann asks us to make a momentary slowing up, the pianist has it at 31 and at 49 when he plays alone

the singer does the same at 39

and again at 55 as seen in Example 2, but always after these *ritardandi* the accompanist resumes the flowing *tempo* in the immediate bar following.

The last ten bars of the song are different in character and shape. This is logical, for their message having at last been interpreted, the leaves cease their rustling. The slightly tremulous undercurrent is no longer there; the voice and piano parts sink soothingly in pitch as the singer says, 'The maiden hears and smiles in her dream.'

Any accompanist who imagines his task in this song requires no thought is vastly mistaken. His little theme (Ex. 1) is gently heard over the soft *legato arpeggiandi*; it must not be 'rubbed in' or, coming so often, it will grate unpleasingly on the ear of a discerning listener and become monotonous. His tone floats without any suggestion whatsoever of percussiveness.

This song has been the darling of sopranos for many years. Elisabeth Schumann sang it exquisitely and today Irmgard Seefried gives us equal pleasure.

Published by Peters

G	D1824	Elisabeth Schumann
G	EW8	Julia Culp
P	R020297	Richard Tauber (Percy Kahn)
PD	23105	Lula Mysz-Gmeiner
PD	19924	Leo Slezak
P	9279	Emmy Bettendorf
IRCC	1	Geraldine Farrar
G	DA4427	Karl Erb (Bruno Seidler-Winkler)
G	DB2957	Marian Anderson (Kosti Vehanen)
G	DA4809	Charles Panzéra
V	11-9173	Marian Anderson (Franz Rupp)
O	188733	Ninon Vallin
G	DA1123	Vanni-Marcoux
PD	66434	Fritz Soot
C	LB122	Elisabeth Schwarzkopf (Gerald Moore)
D	M619	Anton Dermota (Hilda Dermota)
V	81049	Marcella Sembrich
Voc	A0215	Elena Gerhardt
V	81024	Johanna Gadski
G	DB21457	Victoria de los Angeles (Gerald Moore)
IRCC	211	Florence Easton (L. Hodges)
T	A2233	Erna Sack (Michael Raucheisen)
P	R020071	Lotte Lehmann
G	B3751	Elsie Suddaby

ZWEI VENETIANISCHE LIEDER

Words by THOMAS MOORE   *Music by* ROBERT SCHUMANN
No. 1   *Op. 25*

THE first of the two Venetian songs tells of the shadowy passenger in the gondola urging his gondolier, at dead of night, to make no noise with his oar as they glide over the lagoon. None must perceive them save her towards whom they are speeding. 'Ah,' says the lover as they approach the lady's balcony, 'if only we took as much trouble to please the gracious heavens above as we take to please a woman, what angels we would be.' Although we have no reason for supposing that the gondolier's interest in the matter is other than professional it is he who is the recipient of the lover's confidences, it is he who waits and keeps watch below, after the young man has disappeared through the window to have talk with his lady. The song ends without the young lover emerging, but we can picture him in the cold grey light of dawn being rowed back to his wife and family by the ever-patient gondolier. How fitting that the role of the gondolier, in this song, should be given to the accompanist, that monument of unselfish discretion.

The accompanist must bear in mind that the singer keeps to *piano* and *pianissimo* throughout the song and his piano part is just a background. The swaying figure is felt rather than heard, the *crescendo* on bars 8 and 40 and 48 applies to the singer only. The charm of this song

Ex. 1

will be realized if the performers obey Schumann's instructions to the letter. 'Heimlich streng im Takt' (secretly, strictly in time). Here in the accompaniment is the gentle rocking of the boat and the rhythmical swing of the oar.

Our passenger, as I have said, never allows his tone to rise above *piano* for he is whispering to his gondolier. His words will carry, however, if he realizes that a barcarole is not a berceuse. The rocking rhythm is not that of a cradle song and it is not to be performed lazily or sleepily. While the tone remains *piano* or *pianissimo* the mouth and lips shoot out the words energetically. This cannot be done by immobility of mouth and jaw. The expressions 'energy' and *'fortissimo'* are not synonymous, and softly though he be singing, the singer must be sizzling with suppressed excitement and urge. The effect of a sibilant whisper can be obtained by making the 's' and 't' sounds, very clearly. In the line 'die Flut vom Ruder sprüh'n so leise lass, dass sie uns nur vernimmt, zu der wir zieh'n!' there are no fewer than nine sibilants and these should predominate for they suggest at once the swish of the water and the stage whisper of the lover. The song abounds with such examples; here is another; 'er spräche vieles wohl von dem, was Nachts die Sterne schau'n'.

The word 'leis' (*leise*—softly) is an onomatopaeic word, the 's' sound in it, if lingered on (like the 'sh' in the English word 'hush'), imposes silence. In bars 10 and 11 Schumann has made *staccato* signs as seen in Example 1. The notes, however, are long minims not crotchets. What, then, did Schumann mean? Possibly that a portion of the minim should be occupied by the softly hissing consonant; written out it would appear to be something like this:

Ex. 2

so that the 'ssss' takes up the second beat of bars 10 and 11.

The word 'leis' rhymes with the English word 'Nice'; it has, as Harry Plunket Greene would say, an implied diphthong, but singing the word on a sustained note we hear 'na(h)—eece' or 'na(w)—eece' which is not nice at all. The word 'leis' similarly becomes a word of two syllables. But the vowel is 'i' as in 'ice' not 'ah' or 'aw'. Since 'leis' comes eight times in the first verse it will be ludicrous if we hear the singer say 'la(h)—eece' or 'la(w)—eece', moreover the word will be robbed of its charm and intent. The singer can avoid all this by putting the vowel 'i' in the same spot as he has put the consonant 'l'; that is, just behind his upper front teeth. Singing it in this position, his mouth spread in a wide smile showing all his teeth (the front ones only,

of course), the singer can get from here to the consonant 's' without the
noticeable intrusion of the second syllable 'ee'.

In bars 20 to 28 the voice and accompaniment become, if possible,
softer than before. The writing looks square-cut and ugly, but in fact
it is delightfully impudent and charming if performed according to
Schumann's markings.

Ex. 8

The accompanist uses the soft but not the sustaining pedal; his chords
should be unsubstantial—they should bounce in perfect rhythm with
the singer. The gondolier no longer swings his oar in this little section—
he is pausing, either for a breather or out of politeness to his passenger's
confidences. The *ritardando* only applies to bar 24. In Example 3 the
reader will notice the slightest *ritenuto* marked on the first beat of bar 20.
This is my own and it seems instinctive for me to make this—finishing
off the old rhythm with a curve before starting the new.

The close of each verse is so charming that I reproduce it here.

Ex. 4

Each step up, on the part of the singer and accompanist becomes lighter
and lighter. The singer's last note is *pianissimo* in the extreme, in fact
in the second verse his final 'sacht' is barely audible. The pianist will
be hard put to it to match his partner's *mezza voce* but he must do so to
remain in the character of the song; for the gondolier, had he created any
disturbance, would have jeopardized his chances of 'un grande regalo'.

Published by Peters

ZWEI VENETIANISCHE LIEDER

Words by THOMAS MOORE   *Music by* ROBERT SCHUMANN

No. 2   *Op. 25*

I LIKE Schumann's two Venetian songs sung as a pair with no applause between them. Of course they can be sung separately—Mendelssohn, in fact, composed a setting to 'Wenn durch die Piazzetta' without touching 'Leis' rudern hier'. It is only by a stretch of the imagination that we can call the second song a continuation of the first, but its lively confidence makes an admirable foil after the clandestine nervousness of the other. Again, the final 'sacht' of 'Leis' rudern hier' leaves us more or less suspended in mid-air, halfway between the balcony and the boat, while the second song brings us into the presence of the lady whose charms, let us say, have drawn the enthusiastic serenader out into the night and prevented the overworked gondolier from going home to his bed.

If we expect to see an abduction or elopement we shall be disappointed. All our hero says in effect is that at night he will come for his dearest Ninette and together—she in her mask, he as a gondolier—they will float away over the silent lagoon. It is all very proper and inconclusive. Mendelssohn's setting, sentimental and earnest, with its soft pleading, suggests that the singer is really in love, but Schumann on the other hand, gives us a young man who makes love like the average tenor in an operatic role, more concerned with his own posturings—the right hand stretched invokingly towards the audience —than with the lady of his supposed passion; a lover full of *joie de vivre*, full of gusto rather than passion, enjoying adventure for adventure's sake.

Ex.1 *Munter, zart*

175

Scintillating with vivacity and gaiety, the introduction is marked 'Munter' (lively) and 'zart' (sensitive). The syncopated left hand gives impetuosity, while the right with its gay impudence and curvets suggests great play with a cloak; a plumed hat brushing the floor in the most elaborate of bows.

The singer must be impatient for his entry at bar 8. It is better for him to anticipate his beat on 'Wenn' than to be a fraction late, and the accompanist makes no slackening in the *tempo* leading to the vocal entry.

Ex. 2

In bar 9 the semiquaver is as brisk and snappy as possible. Bars 9 to 16 are lively in the extreme and the accompaniment, although a 'vamping' figure, should be energetic. The hands do not fall on to the notes, they spring up into the air from the keys as if the latter were red hot. No sustaining pedal is wanted.

Becoming quite sentimental at 21 to 24 of each verse, the singer makes full use of the *ritardando* mark and sings the phrase *legato*.

Ex. 3

He can make a *portamento* from the F sharp to the B on the first syllable of 'Venus' while in the second verse he makes the *portamento* on 'leben' almost heavy with sentimentality. It is too good to be true and should be overdone.

The piano postlude at the end of each verse is in the same style as the introduction. After the *ritardando* (22 to 24) it does not strike the old lively *tempo* until the first beat (left hand) of 25.

The *fermata* on the last quaver of 24 is mine, as is the quaver rest in the left hand (Schumann's marking gives this chord a minim's length) for it is charming to hear the suspended A in the treble ringing by itself before the bouncing rhythm is resumed at 25. Elena Gerhardt told me that Nikisch always made the singer's B natural on the last syllable of 'firmament' (verse 1) and 'flieh'n' (verse 2) clash with this high A in the pianoforte. He did it by bringing this A earlier on to the scene in the following way. It sounds extremely saucy.

Bars 25 to the end are played without the semblance of a *rallentando*, in fact I make the slightest *accelerando* in 31 and 32.

In my opinion the whole song should be sung with swagger and polite braggadocio.

Published by Peters

THE PIBROCH

Words by MURDOCH MACLEAN   *Music by* C. V. STANFORD
(From 'Songs of a Roving Celt')   *Op. 157*

WHEN I was a youngster in my early twenties and knew everything, I considered it extremely chic to dismiss Hubert Parry and Charles Villiers Stanford with a shrug of the shoulders as too Victorian to be tolerated. Maturity has had a broadening effect (naturally I am speaking metaphorically) and I ceased to air my opinion when I heard John McCormack singing Parry's 'Jerusalem' and digested Alec Robertson's appreciation of 'A Lover's Garland'; when I heard Plunket Green and later Kathleen Ferrier singing Stanford's 'Fairy Lough',

178

Roy Henderson singing 'A Soft Day' and 'The Pibroch'. At their best, these composers wrote some extremely fine songs which can be sung and heard today with pleasure.

Even to a Sassenach there is something which sets the blood tingling in the skirl of the bagpipes and all through this song we get a very plausible imitation on the piano of this thrilling martial sound.

Two Scotsmen—far from home or at the very least, south of the border—hear the nostalgic call of the pipes and we are told in picturesque language what this call means to a Celt and how, finally, its summons must be obeyed.

In the two-bar introduction, played very softly, can be heard the bagpipes coming from afar and it can be seen how the vocal line conforms perfectly with the natural speech rhythm.

I think that Stanford's *mezzoforte* for the singer is a little overdone, for the speaker is calling his companion's attention to the sound of the pibroch and he does not want to drown it by his own voice. The enunciation and rhythm are most energetic, but the tone soft especially in view of the big *crescendi* on 'There's battle's roar by sea and shore and tramp of marching men in it'—'strength of kings defied in it'— 'Vengeance crying yet in it', &c. &c. The singer's main considerations must be to give a feeling of excitement and to make his words clear, for if we cannot hear what he is saying he might as well not sing at all. Nearly always so much vigour of utterance is needed that the singing will inevitably be *non legato*, in fact at a fast walking *tempo* it would be almost impossible to sing *legato* such a phrase as:

Ex. 2

There's breath of moor and ben in it, And sough of High-land glen in it,
13   14

Yet a sensitive artist will manage at 19 to deliver 'dirge of men who died in it' feelingly and with some smoothness. Some slight easing of the *tempo* might be permitted at 33 to 35, 'There's grief forlorn in anguish borne adown the fleeting years in it,' and the accompaniment here has been arranged to help the singer, which can easily be perceived if the Stanford marks are obeyed.

But the most expressive moments for the singer to seize on are from 41 to the end.

In Example 3 every latitude should be allowed, so that 'love'—'pain' —'home' are full of meaning; there is no question of adhering to the rigid *tempo* in these bars and they are *legato* and colourful. Then, after the *fermata* rest at 44—a long one—the old *tempo* and vigour are immediately resumed with the bagpipe figure seen in Example 1; above it

Ex. 3

with mathematical precision and with greater urgency than before (*mezzoforte* now as compared with my recommended *piano* at the beginning), the singer says

Ex. 4

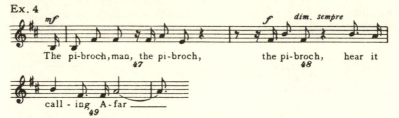

I can still hear Plunket Green's 'calling afar'. He invested the words, without lingering on them with a poignant nostalgia.

Stanford closes with a section marked *poco più lento*, 54 to 61, all soft and sustained, and its effect is the more impressive by contrast with the rhythmical virility of the rest of the song.

To conjure up the picture of home, the singer needs a lovely tone and *legato* line and an absolute *pianissimo*. 'Stars' (57) should be a dream. At 59 it will be a long wait—three beats plus the *fermata* in 58—but this long wait is important, for during it, he is making up his mind to return home and finally the 'let us go' is sung in the same *tempo* as the preceding bars and without *rallentando*. The last three chords on the pianoforte, in imitation of the singer's preceding notes (59-60), should sound like a confirmation of the singer's resolution.

Ex. 5 *Poco più lento*

In Examples 3 and 5 the accompanist will of course use the sustaining pedal, also at 'There's dash of sea and foam in it'.

Ex. 6

A touch of pedal will give a stormy splash to the piano part. But the accompanist should tuck his feet under his piano-stool during the rest of the song. This is most important, for it is as certain as God made little apples that there is no sustaining pedal to the bagpipes.

Reprinted by permission of Edwin Ashdown Ltd.

D M535   Roy Henderson (Ivor Newton)

MORGEN

Poem by JOHN HENRY MACKAY   *Music by* RICHARD STRAUSS
Op. 27 No. 4

I FIND that the quietest and calmest of songs are those that receive, as a rule, the least thought from the performers. It is the accompanists that I indict more than the singers, for the latter seeing a long slow *legato* line realize at once that they have something formidable to contend with, something that will tax their technique to the uttermost and will require a most beautiful quality of tone to meet the occasion. But when I tell accompanists that these are the songs to which I give the greatest care and thought, they look at me in bewilderment and simply do not believe me. I have made the same sort of statement again and again in this book but it cannot be said too often.

'Morgen' is one of Richard Strauss's most delicate jewels and should be labelled 'Fragile—handle with care'. Therein lies its problem, for we paint with the slenderest brush, with refined shades emanating from one tint. Any gaudy hue or violent contrast in colour is eschewed, for 'Morgen' is all quiet (*piano*), rising and falling now a little above and now below this fine temper.

The introduction is nearly half the length of the song. Let us look at it, and play it with the words of the poem ever in the forefront of our mind, telling ourselves that we are wandering, bathed in the golden light of the sun, down a path where the beloved is waiting: there hand in hand, all else forgotten, we gaze into each other's eyes in unspeakable joy and bliss. All is peace and serenity.

Ex.1 *Langsam*

If this music means anything to the artists they will give it all their concentration and love from the very first note, their guiding thought being that time, as measured by the clock, does not exist: there is no hurry. It would be an outward and visible sign of insincerity if one saw the accompanist's hands making graceful passes in the air. No, his hands do not appear to move at all so that the audience is not aware of any movement on the stage. Listening, absorbed, the singer stands like a statue with eyes closed. It is easy to disturb the stillness by shortening a rest or a sustained note, and performers are continually committing this offence through carelessness or self-consciousness. Great self-control is wanted to conquer this weakness; in the above example I have used crosses to mark the places where the song's repose is so often and so easily jarred.

It will be observed that the unfortunate beat to suffer is always the fourth, but this only applies to the introduction, for we shall see later that the singer can be more impartial than her partner and is open to more temptation where this shortening of a beat is concerned. In point of fact it is the very beat we are so apt to shorten that should be prolonged. This lengthening is only fractional and for his part the pianist will prevent exaggeration by making sure his melody sings sustainedly from one note to the next; making, as Strauss has marked, one long phrase.

Phrase 1 to 4 is an upward one, and we wait at the top of it before starting the downward curve 5 to 8, and bar 8 is a very soft resting place where we dwell, so as to give more point to the crown of the arch. It seems ages before we leave bar 12 preparatory to making that gracious descending curve which brings in the singer. Yet these curves or inflexions—all drawn delicately—are made by the melody, not by the always feathery accompaniment. Earlier I said that the melody sings, but this might lead the reader astray, for a conventional 'singing pianoforte tone' is not desirable. The upper sustained notes are depressed carefully and tenderly; they give the impression of a singing tone only by contrast to the harp-like arpeggios underneath them.

At bar 16 the pianist begins a repetition of the pattern he had from 1 to 15 only now he is joined by the voice, where the singer's thoughts become articulate. Having shared these thoughts with her during the thirteen bars of introduction we are not surprised by her seeming to start in the middle of a sentence, 'And tomorrow the sun will shine again': it all seems so natural and inevitable, especially if the singer, matching her tone to the pianoforte's whisper, lets her tone grow out of the alto G sharp in the accompaniment bar 14. It is as if she were weaving an improvised *obligato* round the now familiar pattern. She sings an even *pianissimo* without rise or fall, without any sophisticated striving after effect. The music is all there on the printed page and speaks for itself, if we allow it.

Ex. 2

Once again the crosses are warning signals against that tendency to hurry. The accompanist must be impervious to any signs of impatience from his partner, nor should the singer's even quavers be perturbed by the triplets in the piano part.

'Sonne' on the first beat of 15 does not want accentuation: the syncopated 'den' in 17 should not be pounced on—triumphantly brandished. Nowhere is there any trace of an accent.

In two places the singer is tempted to emerge from her *pianissimo* shell, one is at 'Glücklichen' (19) and the other at 'wogenblauen' (25).

Ex. 3

It is, of course, far easier and also extremely commonplace to sail up to those high notes on the wings of a *crescendo*; but by resisting this temptation these moments become more beautiful.

The magical ending, seeming to dissolve into silence, should not be treated with the freedom of a recitative as so many singers suppose.

True, the repeated quavers of 32 are elastic, but the other notes should be given their full value. Above all, the singer must steel herself and rigorously count those everlasting rests at 31 and 34; nothing is happening here and the longing to make an entry before those three beats are measured out is not easy to resist. It wants self-control. Some singers and accompanists are as much afraid of silence as a child is of the dark. Far better to wait too long than too little; thus the song is allowed to sink gradually into ecstatic silence.

As the last two phrases tend to get slower they will need more breath. I have made breath marks in the above example, but it should be remembered that a snatched breath can be disturbing, while a slow deliberate breath is less noticeable provided it is quiet.

I have rearranged the bass chord in 33, giving the right hand the lower A as it relieves the left hand of an uncomfortable stretch. As for the bass in 35, it is better with a small hand to omit the A rather than indulge in a fussy spreading of the chord.

The sweetness of the postlude should be long drawn out, letting the music die away to nothing so that the last cadence is but faintly heard.

Reprinted by permission of Universal Edition A.-G. (Alfred A. Kalmus, London)

G	DB1010	Elisabeth Schumann (Violin: Isolde Menges)
C	17384D	Lotte Lehmann (Paul Ulanowsky)
V	12-0734	Marian Anderson (Franz Rupp)
PD	62714	Heinrich Schlusnus (Franz Rupp)
P	R020081	Lotte Lehmann
P	R020218	Claire Dux
P	R020195	Richard Tauber
G	EG3386	Willy Domgraf-Fassbaender
C	LB22	Dino Borgioli
P	E11100	Emmy Bettendorf
D	F9355	Anton Dermota (Ivor Newton)
G	DA644	John McCormack (Schneider and Kreisler)
PD	23017	Leo Slezak (Michael Raucheisen)
G	DA1704	Jussi Björling (Harry Ebert)
PD	70512	Herman Jadlowker
Voc	B3112	Elena Gerhardt
V	64339	Frances Alda
V	043259	Elena Gerhardt
G	C3093	Nan Maryska (Brosa and Moore)
G	C3418	Webster Booth (Campoli and Lush)
G	DA5504	P. Anders (Weissenborn)
P	62363	Robert Hutt (Richard Strauss)

SCHLECHTES WETTER

Words by HEINRICH HEINE   *Music by* RICHARD STRAUSS

Op. 69 No. 5

'WHAT wretched weather,' says the singer, looking out of the window into the darkness, 'it rains and hails and snows.' A tiny flickering light slowly crosses the street. 'It is an old lady with her lantern and I believe she is going to buy honey, eggs and butter to bake a cake for her plump little daughter who, with her golden hair tumbling over her pretty face, lies snugly at home on the sofa.'

What a contrast to the preceding song's tranquil serenity we have here! This is a graphic picture of vivacity and humorous cynicism. It is most difficult to sing, having a range of two octaves. Much of it lies low in the voice (causing the singer to force from fear of being over-weighted by an inconsiderate accompanist); also there are intervals in the vocal line which need careful practising to ensure perfect accuracy. I have never played it for a singer, always excepting Elisabeth Schwarz-kopf who makes everything she touches sound easy, without being aware of a struggle, faulty intonation, and an inability to obey Strauss's instructions.

A rule which all artists must observe is that light-hearted songs of this nature (Strauss's 'Ständchen', Schumann's 'Aufträge', Wolf's 'Er ist's' are instances) should be sung and played with such apparent ease that the audience is able to sit back and relax without anxiety, an ease which is patent in the Schwarzkopf brilliant recording. The whole effect is spoiled if the listener sits nervously on the edge of his seat, wonders if you will get through, prays for you, and finally sinks back exhausted muttering to himself—relieved that it is over—'By George, they did it!' Technical difficulties must be hidden. This song is a joke despite the stormy dissonances of the beginning, and it ends in the gayest Viennese waltz imaginable. Singer and pianist, therefore, firstly intrigue us in 'Schlechtes Wetter' with the picture they are presenting, and finally charm us with the 'gemütlichkeit' of the finale.

The rain splattering viciously on the window-pane is heard in the first twenty bars of the accompaniment. Every note, like a hailstone, must be felt and the pianist throws his hand on the second beat to achieve the spiteful *sforzando*. Some idea of the way the vocal line is 'blown' all over the place can be seen in the following example.

A breath is taken after 'wetter' and after 'stürmt' but not, of course, on the rests in 4 and 5. It is important that the G flat in 5 should be dead in tune and clearly heard; neither should there be any doubt as

187

Ex.1 *Ziemlich rasch*

to what is happening in 7 and 8 with the accented D flats (a typically Straussian effect), and 'und schneit' must not sound as if it is merely an octave interval being sung slightly out of tune. A question of balance concerning the accompanist arises here. The mark is *fortissimo* but if he sticks rigidly to the letter of the law, the pianist will drown the singer's low note at 11 and cause him to press: to avoid this we make a slight reduction in volume but surge up strongly as soon as the long low note on 'schneit' is released.

But now the spiteful spattering of hail and snow gradually decreases as the pianoforte descends from 11 to 18; the window-pane is still shaken by the blustering wind to remind us that it is still 'dirty weather' without, but the noise becomes a low rumbling in the background enabling us to hear the singer's thoughts.

This is quite a ruminative passage—'I sit at my window and look out into the night'; but suddenly our attention is roused by a little twinkling glow, exemplified in the pianoforte's treble, 32 to 50,

and the singer lets us know by his pointed tone, eager eyes, and his clear fresh enunciation that a mischievous idea has occurred to him. (The hail *motif* in the accompaniment can still be seen.) He gives expression to this idea at 53, and as he sings about the old lady searching the shops for butter, eggs, &c., he cannot refrain from smiling at his own idle fancy. And as he smiles we gradually become aware that, without making any structural alteration in it, Strauss has converted the accompaniment into a Viennese waltz.

Ex. 4

Since this rhythm holds sway during the rest of the song, it would be as well to try to put into words the secret of the Viennese waltz, for it is unlike any other 3/4 rhythm in the world. There is no similarity whatsoever between this rhythm and Tschaikowsky's waltz, or the rhythm of the two Spanish dances included in this book.

Let us say that a bar is three feet long—one beat to a foot; if each foot is divided into twelve inches, it can be seen that the first and third beats are precise, but the second beat is slightly longer, coming as it does a little early.

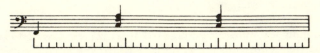

But although this beat occupies more time than the others it is decidedly lighter and must not be stressed. I must apologize here for this description for I am by no means certain that the second beat comes on the 'tenth inch', it might be on the ninth or the eleventh, but at least it gives the accompanist some rough idea of the rhythmical shape. This shape, however, is not uniform for there are occasions when voice and piano move together as in bar 60, or when the piano by itself has three even beats.

Ex. 5
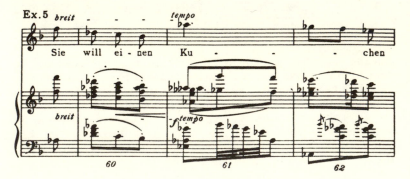

At 60 Strauss instructs us to 'slow up the time', in fact exactly as one does in the opening of 'The Blue Danube', and in such instances the second beat behaves normally.

In any case and taking 'The Blue Danube' again as an example—it will be found that this wayward second beat applies only to the accompaniment and not to the tune. The singer therefore leaves to his partner the intriguing task of searching for the Viennese lilt and can simply tell his accompanist as often as he likes 'No, you haven't caught it yet'—a most happy position for the singer. There is some consolation for the pianist in the reflection that his gay tune (seen in Example 4 and recurring frequently thereafter) must predominate, and a sensitive singer will realize, that where the waltz holds sway, he is accompanying his partner.

After the words 'die goldenen Lokken wallen über das süsse Gesicht' one imagines the lonely watcher rising from his chair laughing at the far-fetched picture he has created—taking a waltz step or two and gradually gravitating towards the decanter.

Reprinted by permission of Boosey & Hawkes Ltd.

G D1951   Elisabeth Schumann (Karl Alwin)
G EG3953   Karl Hammes (Bruno Seidler-Winkler)
C LX1577   Elisabeth Schwarzkopf (Gerald Moore)

AT THE BALL

English translation from the Russian Music by P. TSCHAIKOWSKY
of A. TOLSTOI *by* G. H. CLUTSAM   *Op. 38 No. 3*

THIS delicious song can easily sound commonplace and dull if the performers do not give it judicious thought.

It might be well for the student to allow the strains of, shall we say, the 'Valse des Fleurs' to flow through her mind to help her catch and hold the fervour and spirit of that most thrilling of waltzes. 'At the Ball' should not be imbued with the splendour, gallantry, and glitter of the 'Casse Noisette' piece, for the mood of this little song subtly conveys, as Alec Robertson says, an unease in its broken phrases while the other swings you along with its brave momentum.

But we must never forget that though pallid it is none the less a waltz. If we allow the music to lose impetus, the dancers will sink back on their heels, the movement thereby assuming the slower ampler contours of the German Ländler, an effect Tschaikowsky was far from intending. The structure here is too frail to stand such treatment. To preserve its lilting lightness we should count one beat to the bar.

From Mascia Predit's beautiful recording we can learn how 'At the Ball' should be sung. She used a white tone which at once suggested a shy young maiden dazzled by the bright lights and whirling couples; yet this '*voix blanche*' did not restrict the expressive rise and fall of the vocal line. The broken phrases convey a feeling of excited uncertainty, for a moment they rise boldly then sink timidly; an alternate advance and recoil; the fluttering heart of the debutante who now makes up her mind to take the floor, and the next moment retreats. This cloak of excessive feminity should never succeed in hiding from us the strong rhythmic impulse underneath, for this impulse is always there and must always be felt. The intelligent listener will feel this iron hand in the velvet glove in the Predit record.

While the piano part gives us the rhythm of the dance, it is the singer who strikes the personal note, and it is to her we look for romance and sensuousness. The vocal line should not feel fettered because it moves along with the accompaniment. It is elastic: an additional reason for counting but one beat to the bar. Singer and pianist meet on the first beat of each bar, of course, but what happens in between is the singer's business; in other words, relying on the piano's steady pulse, the singer can spin and weave a line, sometimes stretching a phrase, sometimes contracting, which need not stick slavishly quaver by quaver to the accompaniment. Imagine singing strictly in time the following:

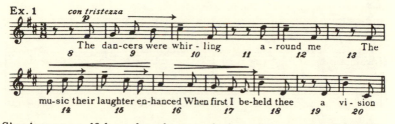

Sing it to yourself, beat three beats to the bar with your right hand like a conductor of a brass band. Then without quickening the basic *tempo* conduct yourself to one beat in the bar—beating the time with a loose arm and wrist. Immediately possibilities of *rubato* and flexibility within the basic *tempo* become apparent. I have attempted to sketch the way *rubato* might be used in the above example. It would be well for the student to remember that the preference here for one beat to the bar does not presuppose a faster basic *tempo* than would three beats, it merely allows more elasticity and movement.

We are caught up in the whirl of the waltz from the introduction's very first bar and the accompanist thinks of muted, but none the less singing strings.

My suggestion in parenthesis should not cut the ground from under Tschaikowsky's long *crescendo* and *diminuendo* but I feel that the uplift on 5 needs a little more singing than 4; the 'cellos at 6, 7, 8 want to be heard. Note too the *pizzicato* at 24, 25 and the sudden urgency at 46 and 50 and the 'cellos moving in contrary motion to the voice at bars 39, 40, 41, &c.

Ex. 4

These little points of interest and charm and more besides can be found; their recognition by the performers will add spice to the song.

That this simple accompaniment requires imaginative handling let there be no doubt. Not only do we accompanists strive to match the singer's fancy, we must also move along sensitively and airily to give our partner a complete feeling of freedom, and avoid, at all costs, treading on her toes.

Reprinted by permission of the publishers, Chappell & Co. Ltd.

G	DA1325	Povla Frijsh
PD	23106	Lula Mysz-Gmeiner
G	DB892	Leonid Sobinoff
P	R02L549	Richard Tauber
G	DA1941	Mascia Predit (Gerald Moore)
D	M633	Gérard Souzay (Irene Aitoff)
Sch	5512	Nina Koshetz (self-acc.)
G	EG897	Ursula van Diemen
P	R20376	Vladimir Rosing (H. Gellhorn)
C	72360D	I. Petna
V	11-0020	M. Kurenko (S. Tarnowsky)

SILENT NOON

Words by D. G. ROSSETTI   *Music by* R. VAUGHAN WILLIAMS

UNFORTUNATELY this lovely song frequently shares, in common with such a song as Schubert's 'Ständchen', the fate of popularity. There must be hundreds of singers all over the world who have sung 'Silent Noon' hundreds of times in public; they know it as well as they know the back of their own hand. This familiarity certainly does not breed contempt, it is too well loved for that, but it sometimes breeds carlessness or inattention on the part of the performers. I am all for allowing the music to speak for itself as I have said again and again in these pages but I have never suggested that there was ever a moment when the singer could afford to allow his vigilance to relax, could afford to cease listening critically to what he is doing. The singer takes too much for granted, no matter how fine the quality of his voice, who lulls his conscience with the sanguine belief that he only has to open his mouth for a miracle to happen. The very fact that most of his audience know the song almost as well as he does, should put the performer on his mettle.

To those who insist that English is an impossible language to sing I prescribe a dose of 'Silent Noon'. 'Open in the long fresh grass' . . . 'look through like rosy blooms' . . . 'gleams and glooms' . . . 'golden king-cup fields' . . . here are vowels and refreshing consonants that it is a joy to give voice to. These jewels bedeck the vocal line, a line of noble breadth never absent for long in any Vaughan Williams' work, and they give the singer pride in his language. At least they should thus inspire the singer; how much or how little they do so is a measure of the singer's discrimination.

'Silent Noon' is all serenity and peace. Its demands on the singer of taste are, in the first place, straightforward: he must sing smoothly and pronounce his words clearly. But the fine artist does that without conscious effort as the result of years of study; it would be impossible for him to sing it *non legato*, for his diction to be slovenly. Listening to Heddle Nash or to Harold Williams, one is aware that they do more than this. I would say that their concentration was fixed on gradation of tone.

They would draw their *crescendi* and *diminuendi* very finely so that 4 and 5, 7 and 8 would only rise a little above the general *mezzoforte*; the *pianissimo* on 'Your eyes' would not be *subito* but would have been prepared by the gradual softening of 'blooms'; the bigger *crescendo* up to 'scatter and amass' would again be made by slow degrees. In fact they would treat the song instrumentally, imagining perhaps a violinist coping with each phrase in one bow. Not once should we be surprised, much less startled, by violent contrasts or sharp points, for there are no angles or edges; everything is curved.

Ex. 1 *Largo sostenuto*

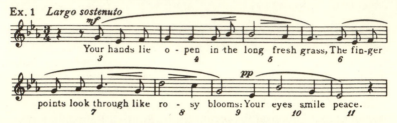

Let it not be supposed that the fulfilment of these recommendations is easy: the phrases are long and must be held out. When we hear a singer exaggerating the nuances, piling Ossa on Pelion, it is not only his lack of taste we deplore, his breath support is suspect also. This treatment has often, in my experience, robbed the very first page of beauty before we were fairly launched; we hear a great wave of tone on the *crescendi* in 4 and 7 followed by correspondingly steep *diminuendi*.

The gaudy effects I have mentioned are doubly objectionable if attended by distortion of vowels; thus we sometimes hear 'lawng fresh grass' and lazy 'O's' on 'rosy blooms'. I would like to point out that the two 's's' of 'eyes smile' (10) are not separated, so that we do not hear 'eyeser smile' but 'eyessmile'; these words would run into one another in speech and they should in song. Again 'inarticulate hour' (66), the last syllable of 'inarticulate' should be pronounced 'let' otherwise the listener will hear 'late hour'.

There is a tendency to make some of the quavers in this song too solid: this makes the music undesirably square. Without departing from the *largo sostenuto* or depriving the utterance of earnestness these quavers must be supple. As he sings the quavers in 3, the singer is thinking of the word 'open'; at the quavers in 6, his mind is on the word 'through'. This 'forward-thinking' gives the music movement without actually quickening the *tempo*. No matter how slowly a piece of music is performed it must have impulse. Thus a singer with an eye for country, looking well ahead, will avoid taking a breath at 57.

He will be silent during that rest but, I repeat, he will not breathe. It is better for him if he cannot do the huge phrase in one sweep to breathe after 'So' (53–54) but the accompanist can help here by seeing that his two quavers (first beat of 57) are not lethargic but are on the move, urging.

This urge from the accompanist plays a big part in the whole song even in the *Quasi Recitative* section.

Alec Robertson, one of the finest musicians I know, insists that this section must and can all be done in one breath, and I agree that would be the ideal way to perform it. Certainly if you were reciting those words it would not make sense, nor would it be necessary, to pause in order to refill your lungs. On the other hand is it desirable to sing this recitative with the quick rhythm of speech? I confess I prefer it sung with great tranquillity and with a pause for an unhurried breath after 'thread': certainly it is an unhurried breath for the 'dragonfly hangs' motionlessly in an almost heavy stillness. But at 46, 47 the accompanist does not hang about motionlessly, he plays ever so lightly and floats forward quickly so that the singer comes in sight of the end of the road.

This suggestion of pliability of the quavers is inaugurated by the accompanist in the opening of the song. His introduction should be thought out in this manner:

But I anxiously impress that all this can be achieved without any suspicion of restlessness: the listener should not be aware of the workings of the performers' minds.

Bars 19 to 22 and 30 to 34 should be carefully practised. The composer has made it clear which note he wants to hear above the other notes in the chord.

Technically this is not easy, for the chords are not spread (how vulgar that would be!) and it is cheating, not to say unlovely, to play the stressed note slightly *before* the others. The fingering I have marked is for the stressed note; it can sing out a little above the others if the finger is slightly stiffened.

I doubt if there are many songs more loved than 'Silent Noon'. Vaughan Williams has created a thing of beauty. It is for the singer to preserve it.

Reprinted by permission of Edwin Ashdown Ltd.

C	9805	Norman Allin
G	B2755	Stuart Robertson
G	DA1776	John McCormack (Gerald Moore)
C	DB2159	David Lloyd (Gerald Moore)
D	K1199	Roy Henderson (Eric Gritton)
Voc	K05309	Clara Serena

ANAKREONS GRAB

Poem by GOETHE   *Music by* HUGO WOLF

SURELY when Goethe recited these simple and tender lines it was in the same gentle rhythm, with the same stresses, inflexions, pauses that Wolf has given us. I like to indulge in the notion that Goethe had this very music in mind when he wrote this little poem. If singer and pianist will share my credulity it will not be unhelpful to their performance of the song and it does give some indication of the almost miraculous fusion of words and music. (I am aware, of course, that Goethe in all probability would have detested Wolf's setting had he lived long enough to hear it, for he was not musically discriminating. Even Schubert's settings of his words left him unmoved. He preferred the efforts of a minor composer named Zelter, of whose works I, personally, am beautifully and completely ignorant.)

No composer is so meticulous with his instructions as Wolf. In all the song's twenty-one bars, there are only two where he leaves us without a guiding word or sign, and even these are phrase-marked. An idea of the delicate nuances that are expected can be gained by a study of the two-bar pianoforte introduction.

Ex.1 *Sehr langsam und ruhig (very slowly and quietly)*

All of it must be *legato*—played with the fingers clinging to the notes. Not one chord or passing quaver is the same in quantity as its predecessor. The *diminuendo* at the beginning; the rise in tone up to bar 2—avoiding none the less an over-accentuation of the syncopated C sharp in the left hand; the gradual falling away into utmost softness—all require the most thoughtful playing.

It is not easy to suggest the rose-scented fragrance of a summer breeze by the contact of fingers on a keyboard, but if the pianist is steeped in the poetry of the words, a sweet and tender melancholy will be infused into his playing. 'Frühling, Sommer und Herbst genoss der glückliche Dichter' (Spring, summer and autumn befriended the happy poet) are the words of bars 15–16, and I think of these words when I play this introduction, for in addition to giving me the leisurely rhythm

—these words, and the music that goes with them, warm the heart and may perhaps give warmth to the tone.

Such is the effect of the introduction that when the singer takes up the story at bar 3, it seems inevitable that his theme should be of Nature's loveliness: 'The roses, the vines, the turtle dove, the cricket.'

Ex. 2

Each bar of the vocal line rises in growing enchantment until the descent at bar 6. The singer, while aware of these mounting phrases, is not called on to increase his tone, save for the slightest *crescendo* and *diminuendo* at 4. Wolf knows our tendency to louden as we ascend the stave, so he cautions us at bar 5, where the highest note is reached, with the words 'very softly'.

The suggestion of leaves softly rustling in the light breeze is made in the treble of the pianoforte (third and fourth beats of each bar in Example 2) but it must not be underlined.

On 'Welch ein Grab ist hier'—marked *piano* to the accompaniment's *pianissimo*—the singer will be helped towards obtaining a darkened tone of wonderment, by listening to the pianoforte's big interval from the high chords in 6 to the low chords in 7.

We become enraptured by this corner of beauty adorned so bountifully by the gods, and Wolf expresses this mood by syncopation at 8–9. This syncopation is dangerous ground for the performers and needs careful handling. Enthusiasm and energy are not synonymous.

If the notes I have marked with an X be accented the reflective mood
of the song will be lost. Guard against this. Disguise the syncopation
by *legato* singing; by remembering that 'Leben' though dynamically the
biggest note in the song is no louder than a *mezzoforte*; by taking the
whole phrase from quaver rest (7) to quaver rest (9) in one breath.
(This last recommendation is a tall order and if it cannot be done, a
breath may be taken after 'Götter'.)

For his part the pianist, though anxious to give his partner support
at 8–9, must avoid percussion; he does not give the semblance of an
accent anywhere. The playing requires great smoothness. It is better
that the *mezzoforte* be under, rather than over played.

At 11–12 comes the answer 'It is Anakreon's grave'.

The rest after 'Es ist' (11) is silent testimony to the singer's awe. Full-time value is given to this rest, and though it will be necessary for a breath here, no one knows it, for it should be unheard, made with no movement of the lips. The pronunciation of the 't' in 'ist' will leave the lips slightly parted all ready for the needed breath; any facial movement will break the spell. 'Anakreons Ruh' is whispered and the singer can be given whatever latitude he likes on 'Ruh' with no disturbance whatsoever from the *ppp* accompaniment.

Although the comma at the end of bar 12 is not Wolf's, a slight break before proceeding with the last section is essential. In this silent moment the same delight in the beauty of their surroundings which seized the performers at the beginning of the song again takes hold of them, with this difference, that their delight is now enriched by their experience. Compare 15–16 ('Spring, summer and autumn gladdened the happy poet') to 3–4.

And then with ineffable tenderness 'This mound protects him in the winter'.

Ex. 5

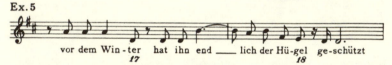

A breath should be taken after 'Winter' but not after 'Hügel'. The semiquaver rest must be observed for it makes 'geschützt' so tender and protective, but a breath would spoil the sense of it.

After this the accompaniment 18 to 21 dies away to nothing. The pianist gives himself scope to achieve a long *diminuendo* by not playing too softly at 18. I indicate how the right hand can help the left in the final bass chord; it must not be spread.

Ex. 6

This pianoforte postlude takes us gently by the hand and leads us away. We go with unwilling steps. Ever and again we turn our heads (the tied treble notes in bar 20) to look back at the poet's resting place.

Peters Edition. Reprinted by permission of Hinrichsen Edition Ltd., London, W.C.1

G	DB(Soc)	Herbert Janssen (Conrad van Bos)
G	DA1470	Lotte Lehmann (Erno Balogh)
PD	30010	Heinrich Schlusnus (Sebastian Peschko)
G	DA1170	John McCormack (Edwin Schneider)
D	LX3051	Suzanne Danco (Guido Agosti)
PD	67593	Heinrich Schlusnus
G	J1786	Bernard Sönnerstedt (Folmer Jensen)
ALLO	AL98	Elisabeth Schumann (George Reeves)
West	WI5048	A. Poell (F. Holletschek)

AUF EINER WANDERUNG

Words by EDUARD MÖRIKE   *Music by* HUGO WOLF

I SUGGESTED in 'Anakreons Grab' that the music was not so much added
to the words but was rather the natural music of the verses. Ernest
Newman, whose study of Wolf's works and life proclaim him as the
greatest authority in the world on the subject, tells us that 'Wolf's is
the essential music of the verses, it inheres in them and must always
have been in them: he has only made it audible' . . . 'His appreciation
not only of the broad significance of a poem but of all its most delicate
detail makes him unique among song writers; none other has anything
like his scrupulous regard for his poetic material, none other so frankly
accepts the poet as his starting point, or makes it so completely his ideal
to fit his music with perfect flexibility to every convolution of the verse.
At his recitals he would often begin by reading the poem to the audience
before a note of the music was allowed to be heard.'

These quotations are from Ernest Newman's *Hugo Wolf* (Methuen,
1907) and I give them because they define with unmistakable clarity
the root and characteristic of Wolf's songs. There is a lesson here for
singers and accompanists which we should do well to take to heart; it
is this: unless we are on intimate terms with the words with which Wolf
is concerned we shall never become intimate with his song. For argument's sake I should say it would be possible, though undesirable, to sing,
play, listen to, Schubert's 'An die Musik' and not be greatly concerned
with the words, without one's enjoyment being in any way lessened.
We kiss the hands of the genius who conceived that immortal tune,
but we know it is 'Du holde Kunst' and we leave it at that, not caring
what the remainder of the verse is about, so heavenly is the music. This
could never happen in a Wolf song. Wolf gives us more to think about.
His music of course can tear our heart, can thrill us, bewitch us, make
us laugh, but—and this is the vital point—he was never interested in
setting words which did not inspire him. He digested them, absorbed
them until they became a part of him, until indeed his music was the
inevitable vehicle for them, once and for all.

We see in 'Auf einer Wanderung' how Wolf laughs with Mörike,
how the music meanders joyfully, with the wanderer gazing on a sweet
little town bathed in the rosy glow of evening. We share the intoxica-
tion of the flower's scent, share the sound of the 'Goldglockentöne'
(golden bells), the song of the nightingales. Joy reigns supreme throughout the song, a joy which sometimes seems almost unrestrained, rising
to moments of sheer breath-taking ecstasy.

Technical and musical problems abound for both singer and pianist, for, as is usual with this composer, voice and instrument each seem to pursue their way independently. The piano part is an exquisite piece of music on its own, but we realize how it is wrapped up in Mörike's words when we hear the singer even though the latter rambles on apparently regardless of his partner.

Ex.1 *Leicht bewegt (Quickly and lightly)*

In ein freund-li-ches Städt-chen tret ich ein, ___

in den Strassen liegt   ro - ter A- bend-schein. ___

The lightly bounding piano part requires no pedal for the first nine bars (incidentally all the pedal signs in my examples are my own, as Wolf does not help us in this respect) and should be *staccato*. The semi-quaver rest is strictly enforced. I mean by this, that there is literally half a beat's silence with no hangover of tone whatever: we are skipping along with youthful zest, not plodding like an elderly rheumatic. This lightsome touch on the piano throws up the charm of the vocal line when the singer enters, for the latter tries to sing *legato*. This is not to imply that at all costs the singer must be *molto legato*, it merely means that the voice part has a line and the piano has not and it is important we should feel the difference between the two.

Smooth singing then, must be evident, but not heaviness; we do not want to miss a word that is being uttered. The good singer, no matter how sprightly the *tempo*, finds time to project his words clearly and freshly to us; thus we hear the first two consonants in 'freundliches' delivered almost deliberately.

The *diminuendo* at 8 precedes a *pianissimo* preparing us for the shaft of light at 'roter Abendschein' where the sustaining pedal is touched to warm the air a little. At the singer's low note in 11 the pianist 'feathers' the keys yet he still has another *diminuendo* at 13 to consider; it is prepared by making an imperceptible increase of tone at the beginning of the bar and the beauty of this thrilling modulation must be pointed by a lingering—of which no one is allowed to be aware—so that we may enjoy it the more.

Ex. 2

It will be seen that the semiquaver rest in the accompaniment has disappeared and from 14 to 27 I find I use the sustaining pedal on each half bar as shown in Example 2: now too the singer finds it easier to sing *legato*, he sails up 'über den reichsten Blumenflor hinweg' with appreciable smoothness while still adhering to his *pianissimo*. To make a *crescendo* on this phrase deserves the death penalty. On the long note at 24 there is a slight opening out *after* the E is attacked, but not before. Nine singers out of ten do not get dead centre in this E, but lodge a millimetre below it, they are not helped by the accompanist at all and

Ex. 3

should practise it, noting the small semitone intervals in 22–23 and the full tone intervals of 23–24. Till 27 the accompanist's dynamics are restricted to *p*, *pp*, and *ppp*, but from thence he begins to cast off all restraint, as the singer thrills with ecstasy at the trembling blossoms and the deep red of the roses. The voice mounts higher and higher (28, 30, 32) until at 35 it drops from exhaustion and, being by now completely submerged by the pianoforte, abandons the unequal struggle. I have tried to indicate in the following example by arrows, commas, stresses, &c. the shape of the *rubato* which I advise using in this and the succeeding pianoforte section. There must, I feel, be some elasticity here. My stressing of comparatively unimportant quavers in 27, 30, 32 signifies that they need more time (not more tone) to enable the singer to enunciate clearly; so often all the listener catches is 'Blüthen beben' —'Lüfte leben', and without 'dass die' in front of them they do not make sense. Moreover the very slight waiting on these quavers makes them a more comfortable springboard for the voice.

It is a glorious but terrific task for the pianist, made the more difficult by the inner harmony in the rushing chords. For his comfort he arranges ample time to drop on his bass octaves stepping down from 32 to 35. He waits on the singer at the 'unimportant' quavers but after that he dictates the shape of the remainder of each phrase. In other words the pianist accompanies the singer for one moment—but the next moment the singer accompanies the pianist.

Emotional exhaustion, his cup of joy being filled to overflowing, silences the singer at 35 and the piano in a burst of marvellous transport tells us what the poet cannot express in words. It used to be said of

Wagner that he took the spotlight off the singers too often and threw it on the orchestra. What he really did was to reveal to us through the orchestra, in terms of music unimpeded by words, the souls of his stage characters; we could pursue an innermost train of thought as it descended from passionate excitement to tranquil contemplation without the singer having to make a prosaic explanation. Wolf does this here. After the mad joy of 27 to 35 you cannot suddenly whisper 'Enchanted, —long I lingered' without some slight preparation. And in this wonderful transition, 35 to 48, the piano does it for us, gradually leading us from one mood to another.

I hope my signs in Example 4 will be helpful; the slowing down at 39 and the *tempo 1* at 40 are important. In bar 40 I play the top of the bass chord with my right hand to avoid a spread which might be necessary if the left hand had to tackle it alone. The one pedal for 35, 36, 37 and for 43, 44, 45 comes as rather a shock when seen in cold print, but this is what I do.

The music has sunk at 46 to a *pianissimo* and now the pace slackens by degrees until at bar 49 it is really slow to give the singer plenty of time on 'Lang hielt ich'.

Ex.5

The very soft figure in 51 played in the first *tempo* does not shatter the reverie, but acts as a gentle reminder that we must be on our way. Even so the singer lingers again at 52 to be gently urged forward again at 53.

The whispered soliloquy continues 'How I wandered here beyond the town, I know not' over the bouncing piano figure of the song's beginning, but now—54 to 62—the treble of the accompaniment is sometimes two octaves higher than the voice, making Wolf's *ppp* sign (at 60 it is *pppp*) very necessary. Indeed here the pianist again 'feathers' the keys, making only a faint tinkle in order that the singer need not raise his voice above a whisper.

However, as if in response to the fresh-rhythmed accompaniment the singer seems to emerge from his brown study with a passage of languishing beauty sung with a tenderness that makes us loth to leave the phrase.

But the sight and the sound of movement, the brooklet's gush, the mill-wheel's splash bring more life and pace to the music until it surges up at 78 with an *accelerando* and *crescendo* ('I am drunk with joy') to the pæn of 83, 84, 85, where the singer seems to clasp all nature to his breast in thankfulness.

This climax catches one by the throat, its effect is so shaking that it does not seem to matter how long the singer takes over it, and the chords in the pianoforte are spread slowly and hugely with the power of a hundred harps. From 86 to 91 the voice sinks again, as if choked

with emotion, and the accompaniment resumes its meanderings which get fainter and fainter as the wanderer recedes from view. Only at 103–104 does he pause as if to raise his eyes heavenwards once more and sigh with gratitude.

Ex. 8

By *con espressione* in addition to the *ritardando* Wolf shows us that the accompanist needs to put his soul into those first two bars. The top notes should sing, always within the *pianissimo*, but in spite of the *diminuendo* in 104 I find it necessary to play the high G in 105 slightly more sharply than is marked to make it ring through to 107. It is imperative that the reiterated chord in the bass be played terribly softly otherwise the B flats will boom unpleasantly. The last two chords are played without delay.

Peters Edition. Reprinted by permission of Hinrichsen Edition Ltd., London, W.C.1

    G DB(Soc)   Elena Gerhardt (Conrad van Bos)
    T A2540   Karl Schmitt-Walter (Ferdinand Leiter)
    W WL5048   A. Poell (F. Holletschek)
    V DM1380   Blanche Thebom (W. Hughes)

ICH HAB' IN PENNA EINEN LIEBSTEN WOHNEN

From the Italian Song Book   Music by HUGO WOLF
of PAUL HEYSE

HAVE you seen a little girl anxiously watching a skipping rope being twirled by two playmates—wondering which is the right moment for her to dart in? Her timing must be exact or else she will stop the spinning rope. With one foot advanced, ready to spring, her body sways forwards, backwards, forwards, backwards. At last she makes up her mind, you can tell it by the tightening of her lips, and resolutely she leaps towards the rope—only to beat a hasty retreat, defeated, as she realizes she has mistimed her entry. 'Now,' cry her companions, 'Now —now.' They never stop the rope spinning to make it easier for the skipper—that would never do.

I have played this song some hundreds of times and very often, as I watch my singer, I see the same expressions of mystification, hesitancy, grim resolve, bafflement, that I saw on the face of the little girl trying to skip. She does not know when to jump in, if her sense of rhythm is weak. It is not an easy entry. Unlike the wielders of the skipping rope, the accompanist cannot yell an encouraging 'Now' to help the singer. It would certainly add to the fun if he did.

Here are the first three bars:

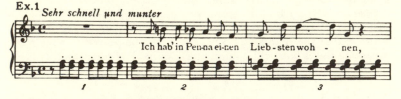

The cause of the trouble is threefold.

The piano part does not begin on the first beat of the bar; Wolf demands it shall be taken very quickly and in a lively manner; lastly, there are no accents to act as guide-posts, the first five bars at least being *pianissimo*, and *staccato* (without pedal, naturally). If Wolf had written bar 1 with some obliging thumps on the first and third beats

it would have been all too easy. As he did not do this, however, it is really necessary for the soprano to practise it a dozen times, two dozen

212

times, until she is sure. So shy about 'coming in' was one young lady
that I played bars 1 and 2 over and over again until I stopped from
exhaustion and from fear of contracting tennis elbow. 'After all, you
must come in some time or other,' I said to her, 'and if you are a quaver
or two too late, what is a quaver between friends?' I quickly add, however, that this is an inexcusable attitude. One's pleasure is heightened
enormously when Elisabeth Schwarzkopf or Flora Nielsen flits in the
way Wolf wanted, lightly and well-poised as a ballet dancer.

Our song is about a young woman who tells us 'I have a lover who
lives in Penna and one in the Maremma plain, another in the pretty
harbour of Ancona, to see the fourth I go over to Viterbo. Another
lives in Casentino; the next in my village here. I've got another one
in Magione, four in La Fratta, ten in Castiglione.'

This young lady's affairs may not take so long in the telling as
Leporello's catalogue of Don Giovanni's conquests, neither are they
such grand affairs perhaps as those of the Don, none the less one is
drawn to the conclusion that she was something of a flirt. She is
irrepressibly gay and sings as fast as it is possible to enunciate her
words.

The first 14 bars are all *piano* or *pianissimo* with the exception of a
slight *crescendo* in the accompaniment at 7 with sharp *sforzandi* in 8 and 9,

Ex. 3

but it will be observed that the latter only make their appearance when
the voice is silent. The same applies to the *forte* and *fortissimo* chords in
15 and 16. I feel that Wolf, wanting the words to be clearly heard, does
not wish the singer to overload the vocal line with tone. She has quite
enough to do, telling the story, singing the right notes and singing them
in time. Her first sustained note is on 'Ort' (14, 15) and here she will
naturally want to share the accompanist's *crescendo*; her excitement
mounts so that when she boasts of 'four in La Fratta' she is *forte*; but
she really makes the welkin ring when she gets to 'ten in Castiglione'.
The top note can be given with all the brilliance possible and she can
stay on this as long as she likes.

Ex.4

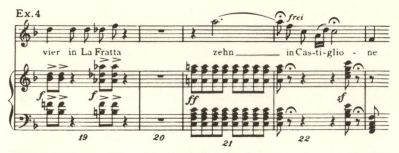

She is left by herself on this top A, for the *fermata* in the pianoforte is marked on the rest. The pianist's hands are off the keys and his foot is clear of the sustaining pedal. A breath may be needed after 'zehn' because of the *fermata* which is coming on the third and fourth beats of 22. This *fermata* is often neglected but it is good to have it, it balances the other long note and is made the more effective by the short dry chord in the accompaniment.

Bar 20 is an important one and deserves a whole paragraph to itself. It is vital that this bar should be given its full value, in addition to the one beat rest at the end of 19. One becomes so excited at this point— and the pianist has his own private reasons for getting agitated—that I always make a habit of counting immediately after the words 'La Fratta'—

'Four, one, two, three, four'—Crash!

The singer will be impatient to attack her top note but she cannot do it until her colleague crashes on the *fortissimo* chords in 21. It is plainly up to the pianist not to come in too soon. He is in control of the situation if he can contain himself and count this one-bar rest deliberately.

Now comes the big moment for the accompanist. The nine-bar postlude is a *tour de force*. The pianist was thinking about it at bar 20, he was thinking about it when the song started, he has been practising it for weeks. He has been looking forward to it with high hopes and a little fearfulness. Compounded of fire, passion, dash, and abandon, it is a virtuoso passage to which even a Solomon or a Horowitz would have to devote hard practice. What a brilliant finale to this little song it makes!

I give it in full with the fingering I use.

Ex.5

The 'breath' in the middle of 30 is a little rhythmical trick; it gives sharpness to the four groups of triplets and it serves to give the player a half second in which to raise his hands above the keys and smash them down with added strength, so that these triplets can be played spankingly and at terrific speed.

What actually happens is this: the audience, having listened and behaved themselves while the singer sang, can no longer bear to remain inactive. They had to keep quiet for thirty-two seconds: it is too much for them, poor things. As the accompanist embarks on his postlude concentrating all his faculties on his task, he hears half the audience clapping noisily. It is all very unnerving for the player. More than one singer has had to raise her hand to quell the uproar that comes from the auditorium as soon as she has finished singing at bar 23. One goes on playing, of course, gritting one's teeth and breathing fire. No wonder Mme. Frieda Hempel wanted me to finish the song with a chord when the vocal part ended: but nobody worth his salt would cut the postlude, even the accompanist has his *amour propre* to consider.

I advise practising these last nine bars of 'Ich hab' in Penna' with three or four infants in the room banging their tin drums and screaming for Mother; arrange too for the telephone and door bells to be rung simultaneously. All this clamour will not approach the din that a few sophisticated members of an audience are capable of making but it may help to toughen the accompanist.

Peters Edition. Reprinted by permission of Hinrichsen Edition Ltd., London, W.C.1

G DB(Soc)   Ria Ginster (Michael Raucheisen)

NUN WANDRE, MARIA

Spanisches Liederbuch   *Music by* HUGO WOLF

IT will be noticed, I hope, in the four songs included in this book—
'Anakreons Grab', 'Auf einer Wanderung', 'Ich hab' in Penna' and this
song from the Geistliche Lieder—how Wolf inhabits a different world
in each lyric, gives to each poet a different style. His music to a Mörike
verse and a Goethe verse seems to be by two different composers so
utterly does he saturate himself in the idiom, atmosphere, psychology
of each poet: a love song from the Spanish Song Book is far removed
in concept from a love song from the Italian; similarly the religious and
deeply felt 'Sohn der Jungfrau' and 'Benedeit die sel'ge Mutter' belong
only and without question to Mörike and could never be confused with
'Nun wandre, Maria' out of the Spanish spiritual songs. It is this
astonishing gift of transmogrification that puts Hugo Wolf in a class
by himself.

Joseph is comforting Mary as he urges forward the little donkey
carrying her: 'Your strength is spent, but have courage, I can hear the
cocks crowing, we are in sight of Bethlehem. I know you suffer but
shelter is near by. Come! Come!'

We see in the pianoforte the little group trudging on and we sense
the desolation of the barren plain. The right hand moving always in
thirds is symbolical of the two figures while the laboured slowness of
the bass tells of weariness of body.

It is impossible for the accompaniment to be anything but *legato*, for
Joseph's feet, as he tugs at the halter, shuffle through the sand. Always
with the tenderest compassion, the vocal line has the same inflexion that
the spoken word would have, that is to say each phrase starts quietly,
fairly low in pitch; as it rises the tone increases so that the top of the
vocal arch is the loudest; it sinks down naturally at the end of the sentence. Wolf follows this principle throughout the song with varying
degrees of intensity as the poem asks for it. In Example 1 the rise and
fall of the voice is but a slight undulation where the singer merely rises
from a *piano* to a *mezzopiano* and back again. The wide intervals in the
accompaniment's bass (7–8) should on no account be artfully disguised;
not that they are detached—the sustaining pedal connects one with the
other—but a slow pedestrian effort on the pianist's part to bridge the
gap between them is desirable: he obtains this by deliberation rather
than accent.

Ex.1 Langsam und ruhig (Slowly and tranquilly)

Joseph's solicitude for Mary's waning strength, his distress for the pain she endures, is shown by the dissonances in the accompaniment, and the singer, even while he sings, absorbs the sense of strain they convey. (See Example 2.)

Ex. 2

Without doubt the entire song is an outpouring of tenderness, but I think even more remarkable than this is the awe which invests Joseph's every utterance, an awe which renders his allusion to 'the hour of your deliverance' as something too wondrous and sacred to be mentioned above a whisper (bars 27–28 in Example 3).

This phrase is infinitely tender, loving, and protective: it is the softest moment of all, the more noticeable by its contrast with the preceding 'Nah ist der Ort' where the singer's tone is more prominent—*mezzoforte*—than anywhere else in the song. A great deal depends on the accompanist's *diminuendo* in 26, it needs very careful execution.

The performers, while recognizing Wolf's meticulous regard for detail, should never lose sight of the over-all architecture of his work.

Ex. 3

One realizes, on hearing Bruce Boyce, who sings this song so tenderly, that his complete grasp of the work as a whole is not obscured by his consideration for detail. Here, for instance, we see in Example 1, bar 6, that 'nah ist der Ort' is on a C sharp, later 'nah ist der Ort' rises, more insistently to an E, bar 15; the climax—if I may use that word without being misleading—comes in Example 3, bar 25, this time much higher and louder than before. Always these words are delivered with the same rhythm but with varying degrees of pitch and intensity, as anxiety grows.

Finally while the travellers recede in the distance, we hear the voice as from afar again repeating

and the footfalls in the accompaniment die away to nothing.

'Nun wandre, Maria' was my first introduction as a young man to Hugo Wolf. It is small wonder that I have been at his feet ever since.

Peters Edition. Reprinted by permission of Hinrichsen Edition Ltd., London, W.C.1

G	DB(Soc)	Elena Gerhardt (Conrad van Bos)
G	DA1438	Elisabeth Schumann
G	EG3498	Karl Erb (Bruno Seidler-Winkler)
G	C3591	Mark Raphael (Gerald Moore)
G	BRM3	Blanche Marchesi (Agnes Bedford)
ALLO	AL98	Elisabeth Schumann (George Reeves)

ETHIOPIA SALUTING THE COLOURS

Words by WALT WHITMAN   *Music by* CHARLES WOOD

AN old negro woman lingers all the day by the roadside to watch the armies under Sherman sweeping south to put an end to slavery. So blear, hardly human, slave for a hundred years, she stands there covered with the dust of the road and curtseys to the regiments passing by, wags her woolly white head with 'turban bound, yellow, red and green' at the flag.

Walt Whitman's terrific story is told over a background of marching men, carried along by the strains of a military band.

Very softly the song starts, for the band is away in the distance, but the rhythm is like iron. The pianist is always conscious that men are marching to his drum beats in the bass, and that his chords in the right hand, though *piano*, are puffed by cornet, trombone, or tuba. A soldier falls out from the ranks, drawn by the rolling eyes of the picturesque old woman, and questions her.

Ex. 1

tur - ban'd head, and bare bo - dy feet?

'Why rising by the roadside here, do you the colours greet?' Whitman now paints the scene: 'Tis while our army lines Carolina's sands and pines.' The second verse is in parenthesis because it is an explanatory recapitulation; a vitally important aside; it is not *sotto voce*. During this verse we are aware that the band is getting nearer as the music swells. Earlier we only heard the distant drums and trumpets but now as the main body of troops tramps past the old slave's hovel, our ears catch other sounds.

Ex. 2

('Tis while our ar - my lines___ Ca - ro -

-li - na's sand and pines, ___ Forth - -)

We hear the jingle of accoutrements by the addition of that quaver figure in the accompaniment's *alto voice*. In 20 and 22 the *legato* syncopation suggests the slight time lag that seems to occur in a big body

of marching men between the front ranks—near the band—and the
men at the rear of the column.

From 32 to 38 the band blares deafeningly. This is an extremely
tricky moment for the pianist; he has to thrash the keys, striving to
procure the most massive sound he possibly can. The composer had
more regard, in this passage, for homogeneity than practicability; it is
impossible in this register of the piano to get a brass band effect with
chords that are shaped to throw all the stress on the fourth or fifth
fingers.

I therefore take the liberty of rearranging these chords in the following
manner:

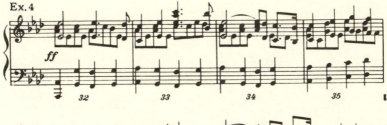

At 41 the entire character of the music changes. In an attenuated voice,
quavering and halting (magnificently portrayed in Owen Brannigan's
record), the aged woman tells who she is and whence she came. She
lives, for the moment, in the past, a past that now seems like some evil
dream; as she speaks the martial music, the measured tread of soldiery
melts away.

In one sentence she tells the story of her life. But she digs deep down
into her soul to find words to give expression to her thoughts; her utter-

Ex. 5 *quasi ad lib.*

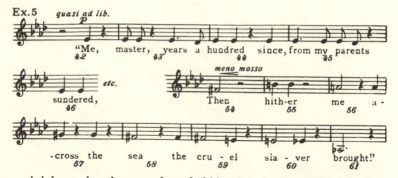

"Me,　master,　years a hundred　since, from my　parents
42　　　　　*43*　　　　　*44*　　　　　*45*

sundered,　*etc.*　Then　hith-er　me　a -
46　　　　　　　*54*　　*55*　　*56*

meno mosso

-cross the　sea　the cru - el　sia - ver　brought."
57　　*58*　　*59*　　*60*　　*61*

ance is laboured as she struggles to hold her emotion in check, especially
from the words 'then hither me', &c. The singer will notice that this
section is marked *quasi ad lib* and should deliver it without any strictness
of *tempo*: he remembers too that he is impersonating a centenarian and
his voice is no longer recognizable as the voice which sang the preceding
verses. His tone, now thin and weak, lacks resonance because it is un-
supported by breath, in fact he deliberately exhales his breath as he
sings and inhales at every rest in the vocal line. It is a dangerous and
difficult section, for this desirably feeble delivery threatens to render
the words unclear and if that happens, if we cannot understand what
is being said by the old woman, there is no purpose whatever in the
song.

Fortunately the accompaniment, undergoing such a complete
transformation structurally and dynamically at 41, warns the listener
that he must prick up his ears to catch this whispered message; but the
message will not reach him unless the singer's concentration is intense.
Tone and facial expression may be weak and pitiful but the lips, tongue,
and jaw are not flaccid—they project the words with deceiving energy.

'No further does she say.' We hear again the tramping feet and the
martial music as the soldier rejoins the ranks and marches on.

When the heat and stress of the day are over and the iron rigidity
of the music relaxes (the slight hesitancy in the accompaniment right
hand at 79–80) our young friend lies by the camp fire, his comrades
around him sleeping, and he ponders over his experience with this
wonderful old woman.

He sees in the flames her dusky face, her bare bony feet. He sees her
'head with turban bound, yellow, red and green'. 'Are the things so
strange and marvellous you see, or have seen?' he asks. This last verse,
in a slightly slower *tempo*, is a soliloquy and is sung softly. The personality of the old slave is associated in the mind of the man with the dust
of the road kicked up by the troops, with the flag and with the regi-
mental tunes and so there is a suggestion in the piano of the tap of a

Ex.6

drum. But this drum tap exists only in the imagination, it does not enforce the discipline that it exacted earlier in the day, but gets fainter and fainter. The fire sinks. Darkness and sleep draw their veil over the scene.

Ex.7

Reprinted by permission of Boosey & Hawkes Ltd.

G B2407   Stuart Robertson
G B10252   Owen Brannigan (Gerald Moore)

INDEX